The Gift of Running

a book for runners and future runners

Dr. P. Mark Taylor

WiseRunning.com

Knoxville, TN

2012

8/1/2012

ISBN   978-0615668604

Wise Running

ATTN: P. Mark Taylor

3909 Sullivan Road

Knoxville, TN 37921

HOW TO READ THIS BOOK

This book is not a technical manual. I have intentionally tried to keep my explanations brief and simple. I have avoided technical terms and explained what I mean whenever needed. It does offer important research-based information, but it offers more than that.

The book is about:

- the human side of running,
- becoming a runner,
- working to become a better runner,
- & staying safe, sane, and happy as a runner.

It moves back and forth between personal stories, quotes from runners, and advice on running.

Most of the subsections of the book could be read independently, but I encourage you to read it from front to back. This is especially true for the inexperienced runners. Read the whole thing first, then go enjoy the run!

This book is the culmination of years of running, studying, and life experiences. Most of all it is about the love of running and my respect for runners.

This book is dedicated to all of those who share my passion for running & to all those who are trying running for the first time.

"On a run, you can find yourself.

In a run, you can lose yourself.

Either way, running is bliss."

-- P. Mark Taylor

CONTENTS

RUNNING IS A GIFT FOR ALL

Running is a gift. It is not just a gift for the gifted runner, but a gift for everyone who has the capability of walking. In this section of the book, I share ideas and quotes that show how running can be a gift freely & happily received by nearly everyone.

*"There is something unique that
running brings to my life:
a sense of community,
connectedness & calm amidst
even the most chaotic of days."
--Mary VanSteenberghe*

A PRECIOUS GIFT

Recall one of those golden moments from your childhood. When you first started to walk and then eventually to run, what did running mean to you? Pure joy. Freedom. A sense of empowerment. I can, so I will. Believe it or not, things haven't changed much since those days. ☺

For those that have not yet found a way to enjoy running, the idea that running is a precious gift might be difficult to accept. What is it about running that makes thousands sing its praises? What makes someone decide to run several miles each day? I recently asked thousands of runners: "Why do you run?"

The health benefits of running are usually the first benefits listed by non-runners. Interestingly, it is often the last one that runners think of as they respond. The more common first responses from runners as to why they run have to do with the way it makes them feel: happier, more sane, empowered.

Here is a sampling of some of the more common responses to the question.

It makes me feel good

"Running makes me happy. The best version of me."

"I run because I always feel better after a run."

"I run for the runners high from endorphins!"

Sanity

"It keeps me sane! Also when I'm running for fun and people ask what I'm training for, I say *life*."

"I run because nothing else stops me from thinking; nothing else is as focused and pure as running."

Empowerment

"I run because at one time I thought I couldn't."

"I run to feel a strong sense of accomplishment."

"Running has taught me I am capable of so much more than I give myself credit for. I live a better life because I run."

"I run because it makes me feel badass."

Because I can

"I run because I can....there are so many people that can't and would give anything to be able to run."

"God gave me 2 legs, what else would I do with them?"

Health

"I started running to save my life. I keep running because I feel so much better. It has made a difference in every aspect of my life"

"I run because it makes me look like this instead of how I used to look."

My friend Laurie summed it up best when she said:

"When a friend asks me why I like running, and it's a serious question, I'll talk about how good it feels, how empowering it is, the sense of accomplishment when you finish a race, the great people in the running community. Running really does change everything."

Well said, Laurie. Well said. Running is a precious gift that is freely available to all who are physically able to walk. Later in this book, I will outline the process to move beginners from walking into running. It is a slow & careful process that has been followed by many. If you are thinking about trying to begin running, there are a few things you need to know:

1. You can do it! Millions have left the couch and started running in the past few years. You can too.

2. It is a process. It takes effort and it will take some time before you start seeing the benefits listed above. Stay the course and the rewards of running will come to you.

3. You are not alone. Running is a social endeavor. Finding people at your fitness level to run with you is probably easier than you think. I cover that in the "Giving Back" section of this book.

Again, I went to the running community. This time I asked for a one word response to this:

Running is so _____! [fill in the blank]

Here are the responses (unedited):

- ENJOYABLE ! :D
- Fulfilling!
- awesome
- Rewarding.
- Challenging.
- self-empowering.
- Empowering.
- Peaceful!
- Everything.
- AWESOME!!!
- better than working
- Energizing!
- unpredictable.
- Invigorating!
- exhilarating, intoxicating, refreshing
- boundless.
- addicting.
- Lifechanging!
- Therapeutic
- exhilarating...most of the time, anyway ;-)
- Mental
- therapeutic, energizing & inspirational!
- Therapeutic!

Whether you are just starting out or you are a seasoned veteran, the benefits of running are many. Running is a precious gift. It is precious for many important reasons that can help you live a healthier and happier life.

- Running is a gift that you can receive.
- Running is a gift that you can enhance.
- Running is a gift that you can give.

Once you receive it, you can also give the gift of running through encouraging and even coaching others. Once you start, always keep learning and always keep sharing what you have learned.

Happy Running!

E PLURIBUS RUN-EM

"If you run, you are a runner. It doesn't matter how fast or how far. It doesn't matter if today is your first day or if you've been running for twenty years. There is no test to pass, no license to earn, no membership card to get. You just run."

— John Bingham

Like Mr. Bingham said, it doesn't matter how far or fast; running is for everyone. Go visit your parks, paths, & roads. Stop by a local 5K race for charity. In any common venue, watch the runners go by. What do they look like? If variety is the spice of life, running is quite a spicy sport! Rarely do you see the super-fit, top-notch competitive runner. Most likely, you will see people of every shape, size, race, and ability level.

Runners come from every walk of life. Some runners are blue collar workers & others are white collar. Some runners are techies with all of the latest running gadgets & some technophobes happy to remain primal in their efforts. Some runners are people that know they need to lose weight & some are relatively happy with their weight. Some runners are fiercely competitive while others are just happy to be outside on a nice day.

Some are running at a 7 minute mile pace & some would be happy to run an 11 minute mile now and then. Some runners are body-builders or fitness junkies using this as a part of a larger program & some are a bit more dainty and consider this a more civilized way to get fit. Some are goal-oriented with regards to weight, fitness, or pace while other runners are more about the social aspect of running

> *"Don't let anybody tell you "You can't" just because they can't."*

WHERE I FALL IN THE SPECTRUM OF RUNNERS

In case you are wondering how I fit into the spectrum, I am a former high school math teacher and currently an associate professor at a small college in Tennessee. I was a runner in high school and had to quit because of an injury. I ran a few miles now and then over the following 25 years, but didn't really start running regularly again until I was 42 years old. I started again to work out the stress of getting divorced after 17 years of marriage.

That was in the middle of 2009. At that point, I could only run three times per week because of my knees. I went to a specialist and he said that I was born with bad knees. I paid him $100 to tell me his sage advice, "Stay off hills and never run more than 3 miles." Thanks a lot doc! Obviously, I didn't listen. The running bug bit me hard. I am all in and happy to be there. The runner in me that I had tried to stuff down since 1985 would no longer be denied.

Since that time, I have been reading everything I could get my hands on. The goal was, and still is, to learn as much about running as I can. I started out running a few miles at a 9 to 11 minute per mile pace in the early fall of 2009. By early 2012, I had run a half marathon in light snow at a pace of 7:01 minutes per mile and a 5K at a 6:11 pace.

I have to admit that I do have genetics on my side as I have remained relatively thin like my father most of my life. On the other hand, the stresses of my PhD studies and the life of a new professor had taken its toll on my health. I won't tell you exactly how much I weighed, but it technically qualified as obese. Thankfully, I dealt with that issue a year or so before I started running regularly. That was through my efforts to eat smarter. The gains in speed that have come in the last few years have come through consistent effort and through my increased knowledge of how to apply that effort.

WHY AM I WRITING A BOOK ON RUNNING?

Most of what I share with you in this book is not my own wisdom and knowledge, but that which I have collected from a broad range of experts as well as from my fellow runners. If the knowledge already exists, then why am I writing this book?

1. I am writing this book because I have a passion for running that I want to share.
2. The information is out there but it is too spread out. This makes it difficult to learn what you need to know about running.

3. The existing books that I have found useful are often too technical for the newbie runner to understand. I will do my best to keep my words at a level that is accessible to a broader range of readers.

E Pluribus Run-em.

Running for all!

*"In the midst of regular life,
running is the touchstone that
breathes adventure into my soul."
-- Kristin Armstrong*

RECEIVING THE GIFT: A WORD TO THE NEWBIE RUNNER

"It's very hard in the beginning to understand that the whole idea is not to beat the other runners. Eventually you learn that the competition is against the little voice inside you that wants you to quit."

-- George Sheehan

I recently sent out a message on Twitter asking what questions my fellow runners had. I received a few interesting topics that I will blog about, but this one struck me. The tweet from Tricia was this: "what i want to know is how to start from scratch at 40yr old woman"

I followed up by asking, "When is the last time you ran 1 mile? 2 miles? more?" Tricia responded, "ummm..... college 20 yrs ago :0) I walk couple miles day and elliptical – I really did mean from scratch (correct shoes etc)".

Wow! That was a big request. Moreover, this was an absolutely critical juncture for Tricia. She wanted to transition from a walker to a runner. Her experiences in the following month or two would determine whether she liked running or not. No pressure, right?

So here is my response to Tricia. This is for all of the newbie runners out there. I'm not going to tell you how far to run. There is no one-size fits all advice because we are all beginning at different levels of fitness. My advice here is more about the way you see yourself and offers a framework for how to make decisions about your running.

STEP 1: REALIZE WHO YOU ARE

You become a runner when you take that first bouncy step, that first longer stride. You don't have to look like a runner. You don't have to be fast. You don't have to run forever. If you start running, you are a runner. Welcome to the club.

STEP 2: GET GOOD SHOES

Running can feel torturous if you have the wrong shoes. Do not begin any serious attempt at running until you have shoes designed for running. Everyone has different needs, but I will not leave it at that. Go to your nearest running store. Do not go to a sporting goods store, a department store, or a

> *"It doesn't matter what level of fitness you are at; what matters is that you wake up every day and take on the challenge of being a better you."*
> *-- Missie Gregory*

discount store. Go to your nearest running store. The workers there run. They are runners. They want you to enjoy running and they have a way of analyzing your needs and helping you select a good shoe to get you started.

Good running shoes are not cheap, but they are important for your health and happiness. You can go discount or online AFTER you have found your good running shoes. For the first round, have the experts help you choose and reward them for their effort by buying the shoes from their store. The folks in the running store are also a great source of information and connections to the local running community. They know the races, clubs, and other running-related activities.

What other running gear do you actually need? Not much. There are many kinds of clothing and accessories available, but if you are just beginning there is no need to get it all. Let your needs arise and inform your purchases. If the weather is nice, all you need is shorts, a t-shirt, and supportive undergarments. As your needs become clear, your local running store can steer you the right direction on the gear that address these needs.

STEP 3: SET A GOAL

If you aim for nothing, you are bound to achieve that. You have to determine a goal before you can decide how to proceed. A good goal is specific, measurable, & just a step or two ahead of where you are today. If you have not been exercising at all, your goal will be much lower than the newbie runner who has been seriously walking, using the elliptical machine, or doing aerobics. If you have lived a sedentary lifestyle, I strongly urge you to become a walker first and gradually graduate to becoming a runner. If you have been vigorously exercising, then you may be more prepared than you think. If that is the case, then plan for your first 5k.

Important Note: At this level, racing does not mean racing! Signing up for a 5K or other road races does not mean that you are committing to try to win or even to running fast. Most runners are racing themselves; they set goals and use a race to check their progress.

> "To get through the hardest journey we need take only one step at a time, but we must keep on stepping."
> --Chinese Proverb

Signing up for a race just means that you have a timeline. It offers a way to make decisions about your training and a way to measure your progress. A race is also a social occasion to meet fellow runners and celebrate each others' progress. In both aspects signing up for races is extremely helpful. Whether you feel like a racer or not, you should start signing up for races. In fact the rest of the book will assume that you are signing up for races periodically.

STEP 4: GET A PLAN

Do not just run what you feel like running on the days you feel like running. Get a plan. If you try to make the plan yourself, there are two major mistakes that newbie runners commonly make. One of these would be going too far and/or too fast. That leads to injury. The other mistake would be to go too short and/or too slow. Since everyone has a different level of fitness at the beginning, I can't say in this blog what will be right for you. Carefully find your level of fitness and get a plan that fits.

There are several training plans that you can find out on the internet for free. I like the free plans on http://www.halhigdon.com/training/, but there are plenty more out there. Some of these will fit your stage of development as a runner. Find the one that makes sense to you. You can also have a tailor-made plan developed for you by a running coach. A running coach is like a personal trainer, but specializes in running.

STEP 5: FOLLOW THE PLAN

Once you find or purchase a plan that fits your particular needs, it is time to step out and do it. As a newbie runner, your main goal is to just get running. It is not to be speedy; that can come later. For now it is enough to go forth and run on the days that your plan says to run. Just follow the plan. You can tweak it later, after you build some experience.

You must acknowledge that this is a long-term investment. Every little baby-step matters. At the beginning of the plan you might not feel like a runner. At the end, however, you will know in your heart that you have been a runner all along.

One trick to following a plan is accountability. As Tricia said, "Be a loud mouth." Tell others what you are planning to run. You might be amazed how much more dedicated you are to running what it says on the schedule once you have said it out loud.

Whatever gets you to stick to the schedule is a good thing. ☺

Remember This!

Fast progress leads to injuries!
Slow progress leads to health,
happiness, & achievement!

STEP 6: JOIN A CLUB

Fellow runners are your greatest source of encouragement and knowledge. Track clubs and road runners clubs have members of all skill & experience levels. It is a great place for newbie runners to get connected with other newbies as well as some veterans that can help guide their journey. My club has several weekly running groups that meet and run anywhere from 7 minute miles up to 12 minute miles.

STEP 7: HAVE FUN

Yes, running is hard work, but you should enjoy the ride. Run with friends, laugh, joke, share. Enjoy the bonus of endorphins. A good workout will reward you with this form of natural high.

Don't beat yourself up over a missed run, a bad run, or an injury. We all have bad days. Running is no different. If you have more good days than bad days, eventually you will accomplish your goals. You will begin to build confidence as you gradually become a better runner. Enjoy the process!

One more critical thing to know is the walking is not necessarily cheating. In fact, walking is an important part of the process. In my walking to 5K program, there is walking almost every day until the very end. Even in the last week there are still 3 days where all you do is walk. There are also marathon training programs from experts in the field that include walking as a planned part of the race. Nobody will revoke your status as a runner if you walk a little bit. Push yourself a little farther each day, but walking now and then might be a good thing.

23

WHAT TO RUN NOW

If you can already walk as far as three miles but not started running, then you can follow my training plan at the end of the book to move to running.

If you have not walked a full 3 miles, I do not advise running right away. First gradually build up to a brisk three mile walk. If you have been a couch potato, this will take a month or two.

If you have already run a 3 miles or longer, you can start with one of the training plans at the end of the book. I have included plans for 5K, 10K, half marathon, and marathon.

At whatever stage you are at, you should read through this book completely now and read it again at various stages of your running. It will all make more sense as you gain experience.

Stay safe. Stick with it. Get connected to other runners. Happy Running!

ENHANCING THE GIFT: RUNNING LONGER &/OR FASTER

Runners set goals. It doesn't matter how fast you run, it only matters that you keep setting goals and working towards them. I began the book by introducing the human side of running, why running is a gift, and given advice for the newbie runner. This section of the book, however, is primarily for the established runners who have set their goals on reaching the next level on their journey as a runner.

Some goals are about distance. Some goals are about speed. Some are about a particular race and/or distance. Whatever your goals might be, there are techniques to help you get there. I have outlined some general information about techniques for going faster and farther in this section.

> *"If you always put limits on everything you do, physical or anything else, it will spread into your work and into your life. There are no limits. There are only plateaus, and you must not stay there, you must go beyond them."*
> *-- Bruce Lee*

RUNNING FASTER

"The triumph can't be had without the struggle."
— Wilma Rudolph

Nobody *needs* to get faster. That is not where the biggest health benefit lies. Simply enjoying the run is good enough for the basic purpose of health. Once you have run for a while, most of us find a desire to run faster. It is good if you can work on speed without becoming obsessed. The joy of the run should always come first. That being said, once you have a strong running base, speed training can get you to the next level of fitness.

How do we get faster? It is possible to gradually get faster by running longer, but that is more effective for the newbie runner. Once you reach a certain fitness level, the increases in speed that you get from increased mileage begin to dwindle. When this happens you have only one choice: run faster.

To some this will sound like a catch 22 situation; I can't run as fast as I want to but you are telling me to just start running faster. Well, it is more complicated than that, but for the sake of learning I will simplify my explanation. I am telling you to run faster but we will change how far you run so that you will be able to run that fast. Still seem like a puzzle?

The thing that allows you to run faster than you have been running recently is that some of your runs should be in a series of runs at shorter distances. If you can run 4 miles at a 10 minute pace, then you can probably already run 400 meters much faster than that pace. That is the key.

Remember This!

**Doing runs at a variety of distances
and paces will prepare your body
to handle running faster
and move you towards your goals.**

If you thought of running as just going out and putting one foot in front of the other, you are right. That is true with all types of runs. Each type of run, however, has a specific goal & purpose. If you want to get faster, the best way to do it is to do a little bit of each type. The ideas in this article are true for runners at all levels and at all distances. I use this way of thinking whether my goal is the 5 minute mile, which I plan to conquer in a few months, or the marathon. If you are thinking about 5Ks or 10Ks, this advice will work for you as well.

SAFETY WARNINGS

Before I go on to the details, I want to say three things about safety when it comes to getting faster.

1) You should be relaxed & comfortable at any speed. Yes, I said relaxed. You can work really hard and still be relaxed. By relaxed, I don't mean loose and free-flowing, just that you should not feel tense while you run. If you tense part of your body, then your form will suffer. If your form suffers, then you are on the road to injury. Nobody gets faster by getting injured. Stay both focused & relaxed as you do your speed work.

2) Too fast, too soon is hazardous for your health. Exceeding the guidelines leads to injury... and nobody gets faster by getting injured.

> "You find out by trial and error what the optimal level of training is. If I found I was training too hard, I would drop it back for a day or two. I didn't run for five days before the sub-four-minute mile."
> -- Sir Roger Bannister

3) You can't do speed work every day. It is not safe & your muscles need to recover. The newbie runner can do one speed workout each week. More seasoned runners can do 2 hardcore workouts each week. See the section on easy runs & rest days for details.

With these important safety notes in mind, let's talk about different types of runs done at different distances: Repeats, Intervals, Tempo Runs, Race-pace Runs, & Easy runs. Not everyone would agree on these as the types, but that is what I am going with for today's blog. Within these categories there are dozens of styles and specialized types of training, each with their own suggested guidelines.

REPEATS

Repeats are the fastest of the runs, done at the shortest distances. If you are running for more than 2 minutes, then you are running too far to do repeats. Yes, they are that short. Any distance that is less than two minutes could be a repeat. If you are training for long distance, this might be 400 meters (1/4 mile).

- Run your repeats at race pace or a *little* faster. Race pace is the pace at which you could run a 5K now, NOT the pace that you hope to achieve later.

- Be sure that you are fully recovered from the first 400 meter run before you start the second. Walk it off. Carefully stretch as defined in the health section of this book. Get a small drink. When you feel ready and relaxed, then start the next one.

- You don't have to do 10 to get faster from doing repeats. Some people do 4 repeats. Some people do 10. Do what you can do while still maintaining your relaxed form.

- HILL REPEATS – Instead of running 400m on a flat track or path, you can run your repeats on your favorite hill. It should not be too steep, just enough to make it a challenge.

If your pace will not allow you to complete the 400 meters (or hill) in 2 minutes, then you might not be ready for repeats just yet. You can start with Intervals.

INTERVALS

Intervals are a lot like repeats, but have a different goal in mind. While repeats are about increasing raw speed, intervals are more about maintaining your new speed over a distance. Because of this, intervals should be at a little bit longer distance. Aim for a distance that you could complete in less than 5 minutes. 800 meters (1/2 mile) is a common distance for interval training.

- Run your intervals at race pace, but no faster. Remember: Race pace is the pace at which you could run a 5K now, NOT the pace that you hope to achieve later.

- Instead of being fully rested as you did in repeats, interval training does not allow for full rest. The time between intervals should be about the same time as you took to run the last interval. Unlike repeats, you run during the recovery time between intervals.

- Since the distances are longer than the distance for repeats, the number of intervals that you complete in one workout should be less. You can do 3-8 intervals as long as you continue to maintain your relaxed form.

FARTLEKS

More broadly defined, intervals include any run in which you shift to a higher speed for a while and then slow back down to the regular pace without stopping. As such, many forms of running

> "Do the work.
> Do the analysis.
> But feel your run.
> Feel your race.
> Feel the joy that
> is running."
> -- Kara Goucher

can be included in concept of intervals. Perhaps the most popular of these variations of intervals are fartleks. The term fartlek is Swedish for *speed play*. The main purpose of fartlek training is to prepare for surges in effort. This could mean the surge of effort required to pass someone in a race, but it could also mean the extra effort required to run up a hill. If you are training for a race with hills but have no hills on which to train, fartleks are the best substitute.

For most runners, fartleks are short surges of pace on a run with a consistent pace otherwise. When I was a freshman in high school, my coach had the cross country runners line up single file and start running. Every 30 seconds or so, the runner at the back of the line would speed up and go to the front of the line. There were 8 of us in the line and this took about 20 to 30 steps. My coach called it *Indian trails*, but this is actually a form of fartlek. For each runner, there was a consistent pace combined with periodic surges.

You can do the Indian trails if you have enough people. If it is a smaller group of runners or you are running solo, you can design fartleks by deciding on a set distance or time to surge, how often to surge, & when to surge. It is not an exact science. In fact, you can just include a few surges on a run by periodically surging between telephone poles. Fartleks are speed play. Keep the surges short and have fun playing.

TEMPO RUNS

If you are racing longer distances, then you will want to practice running faster for even longer periods of time. This is the goal of a tempo run.

- Run your tempo miles a little slower than race pace, about 80-90% of the full effort that you would use in a 5k race now.

- Tempo runs can be anywhere from 20 minutes to an hour depending on your fitness and goals.

- You can choose to do one or more tempo runs as part of a longer run or have it as a stand-alone workout. In either case, make sure that you run a warm-up and a cool-down in addition to the tempo miles.

- To get faster, seek the combination of distance & speed that pushes you consistently near the limit of what you can maintain. If you can't maintain relaxed form, you are pushing too fast or too long.

EASY RUNS, RECOVERY RUNS, & REST DAYS

Will easy runs & rest days make you faster? Probably not.

Are easy runs and rest days important for building speed? Absolutely critical!

How does that make sense? If you work the same muscle group hard every day, the muscles will get weaker. The muscles need time to heal. Easy runs exercise your muscles as they recover from the stress of the speed workouts. It gets your blood flowing & speeds healing, especially the day after the speed work.

Easy days are the runs in which you ease up and get in the rest of your miles for the week. I define the "easy" pace as being around 2 minutes per mile slower than how fast you would run a 5K today.

Recovery runs are exactly aptly named. The goal is to recover after an extremely hard workout. In this sense, they qualify as easy runs, but there is one major difference: the pace is even slower.

As for rest days, some runners can run every day. Most runners cannot. I recommend at least one day of full rest for your legs each week. As for me, I am 44 years old and moving closer to the next age group. As my workouts have become increasingly challenging, I have increased my rest days from 1 per week to 2 per week. Listen to your body. Rest enough to heal quickly and prepare for more speed work!

Remember This:

**Enjoying running is more important
than being the fastest runner in the park.**

I want you to enjoy the challenge of getting faster while maintaining your health. If you haven't done speed work before or it has been a long time, then go into it carefully and slowly. Stick to the guidelines. Rest up. Maintain relaxed form. You will gradually get faster.

Happy Running!

> *"The long run*
> *is what puts*
> *the tiger in the cat."*
> *-- Bill Squires*

RUNNING LONGER

"Good things come slowly,

especially in distance running."

-- Bill Dellinger

Just as the only way to run faster is by running faster, the only way to run longer is by running longer. The question is how much farther to run.

- How many miles should I run each week?
- How can I build up my mileage safely?
- How far should I run on my long runs?

These are all critical questions that runners at every level should be asking. If you fail to plan your mileage, you are likely to be heading for disappointment, disaster, or both. How far to run is not just a question of quality, but also a question about safety and joy. How do you build up endurance without losing the joy of running? A little at a time!

39

Remember This!

If you are not enjoying running,
you are not doing it right.
This includes your longest training runs & races!

A generally accepted rule of thumb for increasing your mileage is the ten percent rule. Never increase your weekly mileage by more than 10% of your current average. Start by taking the average of your weekly mileage for the last four weeks. When you are planning out your runs for the next week, make sure to not exceed 110% of that average. For example, if you have averaged 20 miles for the last few weeks, you could safely increase it to 22 miles. Running 24 miles may or may not be safe. Err on the side of caution.

Many training plans include one run each week that is significantly longer than the other. Now that we have addressed the increase in weekly mileage, we need to figure out how far to run in our long run of the week. Here is my suggested rule of thumb:

1. Take the average of your longest runs of the last four weeks.

2. If your average long run is less than 10 miles per week, then you can probably safely add 1 mile to your long run each week.

3. If your average long run is greater than 10 miles, then you can add 10% each week.

Please keep in mind that the course & pace matter. If you are running an extra hilly course on your long run, then it may not be wise to increase the length of your long run this week. Likewise, you must keep in mind that the long run is almost always done at an easy pace. If you intend to go any faster, then this is not the right week to increase the distance of your long run.

One last thing about mileage: There is a point of diminishing returns. As a general rule, the longer you run, the healthier you become, but only to a point. I can't tell you where that point is because everyone is different. Some people that race at my speed can run 80 miles per week and get a great benefit. I get weaker when I run more than 50 miles in a week. I thrive at around 40 miles per week. You need to pay attention to your body. Push yourself, but give it a rest now and then. See what works for you.

I run with my head,
my heart, and my guts,
because physically,
I don't think I've got
a great deal of talent or ability.
I started at the bottom
and worked up.
--Steve Jones
Former Marathon
World Record Holder

THRESHOLD PACE

---

*"Knowing the right paces at which to train
can be the difference in progress & regress."*

What is the *Threshold Pace?* Imagine a race on a perfectly flat course with no turns regardless of the distance and perfect weather. On this course, *threshold pace* is the level of effort at which your body can barely keep up with you. If you are running at this level of effort:

- you are still getting enough oxygen to your muscles
- you are still able to metabolize enough energy
- you are still able to remove the waste byproducts of this process out of your muscles fast enough to keep going for a long time without getting backed up

I defined it as *barely keeping up* for a reason. If run even the slightest bit faster than threshold pace then one of the above conditions will no longer be true. If one of those things fails, then eventually your legs will let you know. You will become fatigued and you will not be able to keep up the pace. Your muscles may begin minor cramps as a warning signal. If you get that far, your run may soon be over. Time to rest. Working harder will just cause worse cramps and risk injury. The threshold pace is your limit.

There is no ideal course like the one we imagined, I find it useful to think of the threshold pace as a level of effort. If you are running up a hill, your threshold pace will be much slower. Although it is slower, it will feel like the same level of effort. Since I live in the foothills of the Smoky Mountains, all courses have hills. Some of them are really big. Hence, I learn my threshold pace on flat courses and then try to maintain that *level of effort* on the hills. ☺

THE THRESHOLD & GETTING FASTER

The threshold pace, however is not merely a limit; it is also the key to getting faster. If you study yourself carefully over time, you can begin to understand what your body feels like when you cross the threshold level of effort. Once you get familiar with your threshold pace you can plan your workouts around it. In a study of fast distance runners, there was trend towards a distribution 80/10/10 in the paces of the miles they ran each week. Eighty percent of their miles were slower than threshold pace, ten percent of their miles were run right at the threshold pace, and ten percent of the miles they ran weekly were run faster than their threshold pace. How does that translate to your workout plan?

Run eighty percent of your miles each week at a pace that is definitely slower than your threshold pace. Specifically run these miles *at least* a full minute slower pace than your threshold. That eighty percent will make up your long run and your shorter easy runs. These runs are critical because they build endurance. Recovery runs, the day after a tough workout or race, should be run even slower.

> *"I wanna go fast."*
> -- Ricky Bobby

Another ten percent of your weekly mileage should be run at the threshold pace. During those miles, you tiptoe across the line and but keep crossing back into the safe zone long enough for your body to recover. These miles where you are hopping back and forth at your threshold will cause your threshold to move. You will be able to maintain a faster pace. These miles will typically be your intervals & fartleks.

The final ten percent of your miles each week should be done at a level of effort that is beyond your threshold. This means that it will be anaerobic exercise, meaning that you can't process enough oxygen, create, enough energy, & release it from your muscles fast enough to keep going. Since you cannot maintain this for very long, this ten percent of your miles will primarily be done in the form of repeats.

THRESHOLD PACE AND THE PERFECT RACE

I have heard many times that a negative split was the key to a perfect race. A negative split means that your pace is the slowest at the beginning and gradually gets faster. In other words, the second half of your race should take less time than the first half. This sounded rather unnatural to me. Everyone starts fast to establish a position in a race, right? Many runners follow the go out fast and try to hang on model. As for me, I have always tried to maintain an even level of effort throughout the race. I am not fast, so I never considered having a negative split... until now!

What made me change my mind? Now that I understand the threshold concept, it makes perfect sense.

Going out fast typically means going faster than threshold pace. Going faster than threshold pace means getting fatigued earlier. At best, you will be forced to slow down and manage your fatigue for the remainder of the race. Going out fast means you may get so fatigued that you will have to walk or even stop. At worst, it means cramping so hard that you injure yourself. Not a good strategy.

Trying to maintain an even level of effort throughout the race means that you are trying to find your threshold and stay just a little on the safe side of it. At best, you can maintain that almost-at-threshold pace, which is actually close to the best that you can do. If you make a mistake and spend too much time on the line, you may suffer some mild fatigue and lose some speed on the back half of the race.

If you aim for a negative split, however, what you are doing is starting at a pace that is definitely less intense than threshold and gradually increasing your effort. There is no fatigue until you want there to be fatigue.

Imagine you were racing two other people that had the exact same fitness level as you, the same threshold pace. One tries the go out fast strategy, but you pass him less than half way through the race. The second tries the even level strategy. Using the negative split strategy, you keep that fellow in sight in the first half of the race. Somewhere in the second half, you begin to catch up. When you have a mile left, that runner has already begun to experience some minor fatigue. You don't exactly fly by that runner, but you confidently pass. You know that in the first half of the last mile that you can ride the line on the threshold pace. You also know that in the last half mile, you can run faster than the threshold pace. How? Because by the time the lactic acid builds up and shows fatigue, you will be at or near the finish line.

That three-way race you imagined was between you, yourself, and you again. It was you trying out the three most common strategies for racing. If you know where your threshold pace is, strategy three is guaranteed to give the best results: the perfect race!

Happy Running!

*"The first 20 miles is done
on solid training.
The last 6.2 miles are done
on pure guts!"*

RUNNING A MARATHON

"I tell our runners to divide the race into thirds.
Run the first part with your head,
the middle part with your personality,
and the last part with your heart."
-- Mike Fanelli

Many of us actually store enough calories in our bodies to run as far as a half marathon. Hence, you can simply build speed and endurance to reach your goal if it is 13.1 miles or less. All of the content of this section of the book so far can be applied to distances from 5K to the marathon and beyond. A marathon takes more. It is more than the energy required. It is also mentally challenging. Marathons require careful logistics, planning, and practice to a level far beyond shorter races. This is why I am giving it special attention in this book.

Few things in life are as challenging or as rewarding as running a marathon. For many, just completing a marathon is the goal for their lifetime, on their bucket list. Once they complete their first marathon, however, many get hooked. That was me just a few years ago. My first marathon was a case of survival. Since the moment I walked across the finish line, however, I have been determined to run the perfect marathon. While the perfect marathon has eluded thus far, I did manage to finish in 20th place in a small race. I finished that marathon with a time of 3:27:27. My long-term goal is 2:50:00, which I intend achieve before my 48th birthday in a few years. ☺

MARATHON TRAINING

Marathon training takes some specialized knowledge. I will outline some general principles, but I recommend that you get your information from several sources before planning your first marathon.

Preparing properly for a marathon takes at least four months. Most marathon training plans are 18 weeks. Some of the more advanced marathon training plans go as long as 24 weeks. That is nearly half of a year! Why does it take so long to prepare for a marathon? Because a marathon is so long!

If I haven't scared you off yet, let's take a look at the basic components of a marathon training plan. I have included a section with training plans at the end of this book as a starting point. All of the runs outlined in the Getting Faster section of the book will be included in a marathon training plan. What differs is when and how far. Perhaps the most important component is the long run. You don't actually need to run a full marathon in training. In fact, most experts think that it is a bad idea. The longest distance that most training plans include is *only* 20 miles. I say *only* because it is 6.2 miles less than the actual race.

Why is that enough? Simple. It is not the distance of your longest runs that matters the most. It is the time spent continuously running that matters. Since we do our longest run of the week at a pace that is about ninety seconds slower than your intended marathon pace, most runners actually spend a longer time on their twenty mile training run than they take to complete the full marathon race. It is this amount of time for which the body must be prepared. Hence, twenty miles is long enough.

How do you get your long run up to 20 miles? Gradually, just as I explained in the section on running longer. You will add a mile or two to your longest run each week at the beginning. After a while, you will lower the length of your long run every third week to allow your body to recover.

What about the other types of runs? How do they work into a marathon training plan? A balanced approach blending all of the different types of runs is good, but with three additional guidelines. First, obey the 80/10/10 rule as outlined earlier section on running faster. Eighty percent of your miles should be slow & easy. Ten percent of your miles should be right at your threshold pace. The Last ten percent of your weekly miles should be run a little faster than threshold pace.

> *"I just run as hard as I can for 20 miles, and then race."*
> *-- Steve Jones*

The second guideline for planning marathon training runs is to stop the repeats after the first half of the training schedule. At that point, you are no longer interested in raw speed. The emphasis in the second half of your marathon training plan is moving your threshold and increasing endurance. In place of repeats, do more intervals.

The most popular training run for marathons is called *Yasso 800s*. Bart Yasso (of **Runners World** Magazine) would run ten 800 meter intervals, running 400 meters in between with no rest. He found that if he could run each 800 in 3 minutes and 30 seconds, then he could run a marathon in about 3 hours and 30 minutes. When he could do each of those those 800s in 3 minutes and 10 seconds, then he could run the marathon in about 3 hours and 10 minutes. The exact same might not be true for you, but it is a good guideline. I know hundreds of marathoners that find Yasso 800s to be effective.

Last, gradually increase your weekly mileage, with a slight backing off every third week (corresponding to the long run pattern). Take a look at my training plan at the back to see the pattern. Make sure you stick to the ten percent rule. Only increase your mileage by 10 percent each week. This will give your body time to adjust.

MARATHON NUTRITION & HYDRATION

If you increase your mileage and the intensity of training, you had better make sure that you are taking care of your body! Normal dietary recommendations apply. If you put junk food into your body, you can only expect it to perform at a junk level. If you want your body to perform at a high level, then you must fuel it with high quality food and drink! Junk in, junk out. Good in, good out. Fruits and vegetables as a part of a balanced diet lead to victory. Fast food, junk food, and the usual soft drinks lead to misery.

Remember This

Each time you go to put something in your mouth ask yourself, "How will this affect my performance?" If you don't like the answer, do not put it in your mouth.

While each runner is a little different, there are some nutrition recommendations for marathon training. This is NOT the time to go on a low calorie diet. Running long takes fuel. As a general rule, your appetite will go up as your mileage goes up. Your body is right, you do need more fuel. Eat plenty healthy carbohydrates such as whole grain breads, oatmeal (*not instant*), quinoa, brown rice, fruits, and veggies. On the other hand, it is not time for an endless buffet. Listen to your body. If you fuel up properly all week, then your long run will go much better!

Your longer training runs require extra nutrition. Most of us can carry enough glycogen in our muscles to keep us fueled for at least 13-17 miles if not longer. After that, however, we run out of fuel. The body must then start using other resources, such as fat and muscle to fuel the body. Unfortunately, it doesn't give us a choice of what source and what part of the body from which to take it! Hence, you must fuel up while you are running in order to keep your body working. Everyone has their own favorite source of fuel. Many use specially designed energy gels, some use chewy forms of the same kind of fuel, and some even use more solid foods. You long training runs are the right time to find out what you like. *By marathon day, you should know exactly what you will use and how your body responds to it.*

The days before the marathon require special dietary guidelines. You will taper or decrease your mileage over the last few weeks. Your appetite might slowly go down with the miles, but you will need to very careful and purposeful about what your eat in the last few days before the race. While some runners are not all that careful, to get the best performance, you must gradually increase your consumption of healthy complex carbohydrates during the three days before the race. The idea is to top off your natural store of glycogen. This process is called carb-loading.

On the other hand, whatever you eat in the 24 hours before the race might be carried with you during the race. Carb-loading does not require over-eating. Just change gradually from your regular balanced diet to an emphasis on the carbs and you should be fine.

Hydration is just as important as nutrition. We all sweat at a different rate, so our needs will differ slightly. A good general rule, however, is that you should drink 8 ounces for each mile that you run. *You must test this out on your long runs as well!* Practice drinking at this rate. If it works for you, great! If you need more or less, that is fine. Find the balance that works for you through experimenting.

RACE DAY

On marathon day, start your morning with 16 ounces of water and some easy-to-digest complex carbohydrates with a little bit of protein. Aim for 200 to 300 calories for each hour between breakfast and the race. A bowl of oatmeal works for many runners. Some have whole grain toast. Test it out before your long training runs.

To know how much to each during the race you will need to gather some information and do some math. During the actual race, you will need 0.5-1.0 grams of carbohydrates for each kilogram of body weight per hour. Check your gel packets or other fuel supplies to see how many grams of carbs each will provide. Also factor in what you will drink during the run. Always find out which sports drink will be served at the marathon. Unless you drink strictly water, you should factor in those calories as well.

Remember This!

There is no wall other than the one you construct!

If you drink & eat the right amount you will have 26.2 miles of fuel. If you maintain a modest pace that is significantly slower than your threshold pace, then fatigue should not be a problem. You will get tired, but your muscles should be able to handle the whole 26.2 miles without quitting.

MY MARATHON STORY:
FROM 5:35 TO 3:27 IN 18 MONTHS

"You have to forget

your last marathon before you try another.

Your mind can't know what's coming."

– Frank Shorter

I insert my marathon story into this section of the book to share with you my learning process, the insights that I gained through experience, and to illustrate the points already made about training and running a marathon.

Even though Frank Shorter was a world-class marathoner, I respectfully disagree. I do remember my last marathon. I remember all of them. If I didn't remember, then I would not have learned from them. If I had not learned from them, then I would not have returned for a second or third. The name of my blog is WiseRunning.com. That is not a claim that everything I do is wise. In fact, it is the opposite. I am gradually becoming wise through the school of hard knocks. The more mistakes I make while running, the wiser & faster I become.

I am now in training for my fifth marathon. I have my training plan and I am sticking to it as much as I can. It is, to say the very least, vastly different from the training for my first marathon. Looking back, I no longer consider that training. What I did before my first marathon was haphazard and probably a little dangerous.

- I was only running a few days a week, because my knees were always sore after a run.
- I didn't have a plan, I was just making it up as I went.
- I only ran one 17 miler and one 20 mile run, everything else was 13 miles or less.
- I took a total of three drinks of water during training runs in the entire "training" program.
- There was only 1 run where I tried to consume any calories

Yes, that's right. I didn't feel comfortable drinking while running, so I took a grand total of 3 drinks during the entire "training" program. If you know anything about running long distances, you can probably guess what kind of experience I had in my first marathon. Not good.

In April of 2010, I glided through the first half of the Knoxville Marathon in just over 2 hours and felt strong. By mile mile 16, I knew I didn't feel right. By mile 18, I started cramping a little. By mile marker 19, every muscle in my body was taking turns cramping. I walked the last 7.2 miles. It began to rain hard. By the time I crossed the first bridge over the river, it was raining sideways because of the huge cross-breeze. I was wet, cold, shivering, and generally miserable.

Thank God for nice people! A volunteer under the bridge in the 20th mile gave me poncho. It kept me warm enough to stave off the medics and gradually walk to the finish. It was a humbling experience watching all of the pacers pass me one by one. I refused to quit. I completed my first marathon in 5 hours and 35 minutes. I was in pain & suffering for the next week.

What did I learn from marathon number 1? Plenty!

- You had better have a training plan or you will suffer!
- You had better have calories, electrolytes, and drinks or you will suffer!
- I am not a quitter.

That is the beginning of the story. What happened in the next 18 months? The first thing that I always do after a bad run is to plan my return. You can't let a course beat you. The second thing I did was to start reading. I had half-heartedly looked at training plans before, but now I was seriously shopping for one. I read up on hydration, energy gels, shoes, & everything else I could find.

I did not start the marathon training right away. In fact, I started where I should have started the first time. I began to train for shorter distances first. A couple of months later, I ran the Expo 5K in 21:55, a 7:03 mile pace & almost a full minute faster than my previous 5K time. Next I set my sites on improving my half-marathon time. I had managed to survive a 1:59:27 at the Oak Ridge half the previous year. I began to build a mileage base running 4 days a week fairly consistently, which was not easy because my knees were still ailing. In October of 2010, I ran the Secret City Half Marathon in 1:48:59.

The things I was doing differently than before:

- I gradually built up my weekly mileage.
- I did a speed workout at the track about once a week, running 400m or 800m repeats.
- On my runs over 10 miles, I was experimenting with sports drinks and energy gels.

One more critical thing happened in late December of 2010. I found the right pair of shoes for me. The result was happy knees! When I run in these shoes, my knees do not get more sore than any other part of my body. What a blessing!

TRAINING FOR THE 2011 KNOXVILLE MARATHON

Despite my best intentions of implementing the full Hal Higdon marathon training schedule, I found myself starting late. I did, however, accomplish most of his Advanced 1 training schedule. I started on the Advanced 1 rather than intermediate plans because of the mileage base that I had built. I found that I could adjust this particular schedule just a bit and it pushed me just a little harder. Just right.

The things I was doing differently than before:

- I was following an expert's marathon training plan that challenged me just enough.
- I focused my track work on 800 meter repeats exclusively, running every 800 at 3:30.
- I was taking electrolyte capsules to supplement the sports drinks & energy gels.
- I ran three 20 mile runs in preparation for the marathon.

1 YEAR AFTER MY FIRST MARATHON

I returned to the scene of the crime a year later. I was not going to allow a course to defeat me and get away with it. I was here for revenge. I had specialized training, energy gel, a fuel belt with my own Gatorade, electrolyte tablets, and cool shoes. Yes, folks, I was back to kick some butt!

Did it all go as planned? Of course not. I had rumblings in my tummy before I had reached mile marker 5. Thankfully, the Knoxville Track Club and the race director know what runners need. There were plenty of porta-potties along the route. I made prolonged visits to these facilities no less than four times. That was glitch number one. Glitch number two came when I dropped the electrolyte capsules somewhere in the first 6 miles. Thankfully, I had taken several before the start so I wasn't completely out of luck.

Despite these issues, I still finished the first half of the marathon at around 1:48. The first part of the course has more hills than the second half, so I knew that I could cruise to a decent time even if I got tired and crampy. This time the second half of the marathon did go much better. I took the time to drink more, but kept a respectable pace. I felt my body running low on fuel, but I had energy gel. I felt sort of a pre-cramp feeling, so I chose to slow down my pace and try to relax my muscles. I did gradually slow down more than I wanted to, but I managed to complete the course in 3:55:59 - about an hour and 40 minutes faster than in 2010.

I still felt as if I had been run over by a truck and my feet had a lot of blisters, but I had taken that course to school! It had beaten me in 2010 and I beat it in 2011.

THE NEXT 6 MONTHS

It only took a couple of days to recuperate from the extreme soreness. In that time, I was already beginning to plan my next race. I knew that I would return to run the Knoxville Marathon in 2012, but I wanted to run a marathon before that. I eventually found the 7 Bridges Marathon scheduled for mid-October of 2011. It was just a short drive south to Chattanooga and the course looked to be flatter than Knoxville. I did not wait for the 18 week marathon training schedule to kick in. After resting and some gentle, short runs for the first two weeks, I began the process of cranking up my mileage and speed work.

IMPORTANT: At this time, I learned that the most important way to handle running in extreme heat is to be running long runs as the heat increases from spring to summer.

In other words, in addition to precautions of extra water and electrolytes, you also have to gradually get your body used to running in increasingly hot temperatures. If you begin to increase your mileage a lot when it is already hot, you may suffer a heat stroke!!!

Thankfully, that did fit my plan. The official training plan that I used to prepare for the 7 Bridges Marathon was Hal Higdon's Advanced 2 plan. It represented another increase in mileage and intensity. By this time, I had shifted to running in new shoes that were even better than the ones before. I ran six days a week and felt pretty good.

I followed Higdon's advice and used my marathon training to get some faster times in shorter races. I ran the 2011 Expo 10K in May in 43:09 [6:56 mile pace] and the Fireball 5K in July in 20:41 [6:39 pace].

The things I was doing differently than before:

- I ran 6 days per week & rested every Friday regardless of how good I felt.

- I was following a new marathon training plan that challenged me just enough.

- I was now doing my 800 meter repeats at 3:00, 30 seconds faster than before

- I continued testing out new sports drinks & energy gels.

- I ran more 20 mile runs in preparation for the marathon and even went 22.5 once.

18 MONTHS AFTER THE FIRST MARATHON

I was beginning to fantasize about qualifying for Boston. At my age, it would have taken a time of 3:25. That would have been 30 minutes and 59 seconds faster than my marathon just 6 months prior. At this level, it is not considered realistic or even smart to try to improve that much in such a short time. On the other hand, I knew that I was getting faster and smarter. I thought I had an outside chance if everything came together just right and the wind was at my back the whole way.

Rather than expect a miracle, however, I decided to say that 3:25 was my fantasy goal but that I would be happy to finish anywhere in the 3:30s. After all, 3:35 would be a big improvement over 3:55. For the pace of my training, this seemed reasonable.

At the start line, I was nervous! I couldn't decide between my two strategy choices. Should I run at an 8 minute pace and then speed up on the back half to see what I could do? Should I start out a little faster than "Boston pace" and hope to get close to that mark? When the starting gun went off, I was thinking plan B. I had to take a shot at Boston. If I failed, I would still finish with a good time.

That is exactly what happened. I finished the first half at a 7:24 pace that felt comfortable. It did not feel like pushing it. I drank and ate more than I had ever attempted in previous marathons in the effort to avoid the dehydration and nutrition issues that had slowed me down. I was gradually slowing down throughout the second half, but with three miles to go, I could still run the last miles at a 9 minute pace and qualify for Boston. Unfortunately, that is when I really started to slow down. Despite my best training and my best drinking strategy, I was still dehydrated.

When I crossed bridge number 7 I had no gas left and that is when the cramps set in. I gave up Boston and slowed down. I was disappointed, but I knew that I had made a tremendous improvement and run the right race. Looking back, the only change I would have made would be to drink 5-8 more cups of Powerade along the way. It is just an educated guess, but I believe I would have finished 5 to 10 minutes faster if I had slowed down to drink.

As it was, I dragged myself across the finish line in a time of 3:27:27. I had improved my time by a little less than half an hour. Nice! Next time, however, I will do a better job of following my "perfect race" guidelines. ☺

RENEWING THE GIFT: MOTIVATION

What keeps you running?   This is an important question to consider.   Every runner, no matter how gung-ho, will eventually experience times when our motivation wanes.   What will motivate you during these times? This section of the book offers advice on how to keep running through rough spots and get reinvigorated.

"We've gotta remember the feeling we get after our run!"
-- Jesica D'Avanza

RECAPTURING THE JOY OF RUNNING

"Running is play,

for even if we try hard to do well at it,

it is a relief from our everyday cares."

-- Jim Fixx

I drank some Gatorade Pro, but I didn't want to. I put on my running gear, but I didn't feel like it. My allergies were acting up, I wanted to take a nap, but I was in training for a marathon... so I begrudgingly trudged out the door.

As I was driving to the greenways for a run, I was imagining which course I would run my 4 miles. Hal Higdon's Advanced II training schedule said I should run 4 miles at my target marathon pace. Should I start out by the Earth Fair market and run down the 3rd Creek Greenway. No. I almost always run that. I don't feel like it. Should I start out at Tyson park and run towards the UT football stadium? Nah. Just don't feel like it. Should I run Cherokee Boulevard, where I had "Slayed the Specter of a Bad Run" before? No. I really don't think I'm supposed to run hills today.

I turned towards that one anyway. "After all," I reasoned with myself, "I've got to run somewhere." Thankfully, as I approached the parking lot near the zero mile marker on Cherokee Boulevard I saw something inspiring: the cross country course at Sequoyah Park! I have watched my kids run several cross country races there. Each time, I was reminded of my own high school cross country career. I always told myself that I would run the course and see how I would do. Today was the day!

Seeing the park this morning triggered good memories of my kids and the good memories of my high school experience. I was immediately drawn. My body was a few minutes behind my heart. I was a little stiff. I ran a few hundred feet and stretched just a little. Right there and then, I decided that my body would just have to kick in because my heart was saying, "Go!"

I ran the full 5k course and added 1 mile. I started out stiff, but trying hard and squeaked out the first mile in about 7:30. I started to get a rhythm going and gradually loosened up. I was running in my happy place...caught up somewhere between old memories, new memories, & the flat grassy area I was running on next to the river/lake. I was caught up in several moments at once and all of them were good.

I ran the final 2.15 miles at around a 7:00 mile pace and walked another half mile back to the car. My goal for the day was to run 4 miles at around a 7 minute pace. I managed to go a little farther, on grass, and kept it at an average of 7:08. Not bad for a day when I just really didn't feel like running.

The main accomplishment of the day, however, was capturing the joy of running when I didn't seem to have it.

How do you get to your happy place? Do you remember? If not, then try this. Take a trip down memory lane. Go back to your best races, your favorite runs. What did you feel like? Pretty nice, right? What a great feeling!

- Was it the joy of being out in nature?
- Was it the companionship of a good friend or group of friends?
- Was it achieving a goal?

- Was it the freedom of running when you had no goal in mind & no stopwatch to check?

Whatever it was that made those runs so special can be brought back. You are in control of the variables that can make running a joy or a drudgery. Make it happen. Feel the joy of running once more. ☺

MOTIVATION: GETTING OUT OF THE DOOR

"The hardest step for a runner
is the first one out of the front door."

Oh, how true are those words! Even if you love running, some days are tougher than other to muster up the strength to take the first step. Nearly without fail, you will return from your run glad that you did it. Running gives more than it takes. You will be more relaxed and, in the long run, you will have more energy if you run.

But how do you convince your reluctant self to get up off of the couch when you just aren't feeling it?

Remember This:
Every day that you go out and run,
you are writing your own legend,
becoming your own superhero.
What do you want the next chapter to say?

79

Some will say, "My own legend? Isn't that a bit much for a runner as slow as me?" No. It isn't too much. It is not enough. Millions of people are sitting on their couches, eating potato chips or bon-bons and wishing that they were in shape. They remember fondly the times earlier in life when they were more fit and active. They wish they were in better shape.

> *"The difference between try and triumph is a little UMPH."*
> *-- Marvin Phillips*

Well, guess what? You stopped wishing and started doing something about it. When you decide to go out and run when you just don't feel like it, you are taking command of your own destiny. You aren't sitting around wishing. You are a person of action. Each day that you defeat that blah feeling and passive state by going out and conquering those miles, whether or not you feel like it, you are becoming your own action hero. A real-life legend in your own time, you step out the door and defeat the enemies known as mediocrity, complacency, and passivity.

Every day that you go out and run, you are writing your own legend, becoming your own superhero. It doesn't matter who else pays attention or knows the legend. This epic tale is for you. What do you want the next chapter to say?

Now pick up your cape and boots and head for the door. There are more fitness adventures to be had. You are a running legend. Go kick some butt!

"But it's weird.
Why is something I love
such a battle sometimes
to go out and do?
It is amazing and confusing!"
-- Dan Mott

SLAYING THE SPECTER OF A BAD RUN

I had a horrible run one day and it was killing me. Not during the run, mind you, but after the run. During the run I was merely overtired and dehydrated. That was bad enough, but this bad run was hanging over my head... calling me names...taunting...telling me that I was not good enough. The hills were huge. As I remembered the contours of each hill, they seemed to come alive, grimacing and laughing at me.

How can one run haunt me so much so quickly? Probably because I have chosen some lofty goals and a short timeline. With all of that pressure, I had no time for a bad run. Bad runs, however, are inevitable. We can't control all of the things that life throws at us and we are certainly prone to making mistakes. Logically, this was not the end of the world, but it felt like it.

How did I slay the specter of the bad run? I rested up for a day, I was well-fueled and hydrated, I set a realistic goal for next day's run, AND... most importantly, I set the course for that day's run in the toughest part of yesterday's run.

I looked those grimacing hills straight in the eyes and shouted, "NO! You will not win. I may not be as fast as I want to be, but I am on my way. You will not win. "

I did not set any new records that day, but I did run a reasonably good time for the course and conditions. I faced the specter of doubt cast upon me by the previous day's fiasco.

It made the future look pretty darn good.

> *"Today will be gone tomorrow and while striving for success is a must, we are not promised a tomorrow. Be easy on yourself; forgive yourself and live life to its fullest."*
> *--Crystal Tinsley.*

POTENTIAL, RISK, & FAILURE

"The crime is not to avoid failure;
the crime is to not give triumph a chance!"
-- H. Weldon

The vast majority of runners set goals. Whenever you set a goal, however, you run the risk of not meeting it. How big should the goals be? Some set their goals far too modestly. They train harder than ever before but enter a race aiming to beat their best time by a second or two. That is pretty good if you are in the twilight of your running career. In fact, that would be a huge goal. If you are still in the prime of your running years, if you are still improving steadily, then this goal is far too low. You can't PR every race, but if you are still young you should at least give it a shot.

As for me, I am still in that stage of gradual improvement. While I do not subscribe to the "Go big or go home" mentality, I do believe in aiming high.

Here is my view:

- If you aim for a lofty goal and achieve it, then GREAT! It was a goal worthy of pursuing!
- If you aim for a lofty goal and miss by a little bit, then you have improved a lot. Good for you! It was a goal worthy of pursuing!
- If you aim low and achieve it, who cares?
- If you aim low and miss it, do not be surprised. Your heart was never really in it in the first place.

> "Only those who will risk going too far can possibly find out how far they can go."
> -- T. S. Eliot

There are only two kinds of failure in running. One kind of failure is getting injured because you went too fast for your own good. Your goals should never be so big that they create that risk. The worse type of failure in running is the failure to try. Unmet potential is a crime you commit against yourself. You are the victim and the perpetrator.

Set goals wisely through a careful study of what you have done recently. Aim high. You will not meet every goal, but that is fine. You will make regular progress. You will be able to reach your potential. Happy running!

"Real victory comes from defeating one's own limitations."

RACING AS MOTIVATION

"Racing is the fun part;
it's the reward of all of the hard work."
-- Kara Goucher

If you are running to compete with others, then racing is obviously a part of what you do. If you are running for health or other reasons, you may wonder why you should bother registering for and running a race.

I asked runners questions about racing to find out why they register. This first question I asked was the reason they choose to sign up for races.

The reason that I sign up for races is _____.

- to challenge myself!
- for motivation, most of the time I run because I totally enjoy it, but just below the surface, I still like to test myself against others....
- Supporting the sponsoring charity

- I love the atmosphere! I love running fast and need other fast runners to push me, I kind of lollygag on my own, even though the effort feels the same. Race day adrenaline is awesome!!
- To stay motivated
- Motivation, the challenge, and being amongst runners of all ages and abilities.
- Bling! And generally as a training run with a few thousand of my new best friends for some other race I've already signed up for.
- I love walking, I like cute t-shirts, and I enjoy seeing everyone! :) [*she is a walker* ☺]
- to get more race experience, to become a smarter racer
- keeps me running, helps me set a goal
- To test my training, get a shot of adrenaline, be completive with the clock, and get the shirt of course
- Because chicks dig fast guys in short shorts! Right?
- I need a reason?

- I like to measure my progress!
- To get a medal! [finishers medal]
- To have something to train for
- To stay disciplined
- The reason that I sign up for races is to challenge my physical & mental strength, to prove to myself I can do it.

My friend Teresa summed it up best in her response:

"Races push me to stay focused on my training. Also, I love the fun & excitement in the crowd, getting together with friends & making new ones :) Free stuff is good too."

Those are some of the reasons why they register, but I found out a little more when I posed the question differently.

After I register for a race, I feel _____.

- Awesome!!
- Invincible!
- Excited/Nervous!
- Driven.

- Focused
- Pumped and ready for training!!
- Excited & ready to set goals
- Content that I now have a plan
- Like a kid waiting for Christmas
- Anxious vs excitement...
- Cautiously optimistic!!!
- Ready to go.
- That I need to step up my training.
- Jazzed!!!
- Excited and good nervous!
- There's no turning back (gulp)
- Motivated and break out in anxious/excited sweat
- Committed to my training
- I like the atmosphere that race day brings:)

There you have it! The reason we register for races is to motivate ourselves. It causes us to take our training a little more seriously. We get nervous, but enjoy the excitement of a new challenge. We are runners. That's just how we roll. ☺

AGING GRACEFULLY

"With every finish line I cross,

there are new reasons to keep going."

-- Joan Benoit Samuelson

As we get older, we have to slow down and not work so hard, right? I mean you're not getting any younger... Wrong! You do not have to go gently into that good night. Although there is a point in your life that you may never earn another PR, never run as fast as you once did, that does not mean that you have to give up. You can still set and meet goals. You can still compete with yourself and others.

THE FOUNTAIN OF YOUTH

Eighty-one year old Lew Hollander completes Ironman triathlon competitions. Lew completes 2.4 miles swimming, 112 miles cycling, and 26.2 miles running all in one event. When someone asked Lew his "Secret" to longevity and health, he first just looked at the man with a puzzled look. After thinking about it, however, Lew decided that his "secret" to success was anaerobic exercise.

Anaerobic exercise is not what you do in the Ironman. Anaerobic exercise means that you do not have enough oxygen to do the exercise for very long. It is short burst of strength and speed. Lew does not swim, bike, or run that far in his training. He attributes his continued ability to complete Ironman triathlons to a combination of aerobic and anaerobic exercises.

Likewise, I saw the story of Ernestine Shepherd, the 75 year old bodybuilding instructor. Yes, she runs ten miles a day which is an aerobic exercise. What got her going and keeps her going, however, is the anaerobic work. She was a prissy girl growing up but by 71, she did not like the state of her health. At age 71, she decided to take up competitive bodybuilding. Her main activity is weightlifting. It is a combination of aerobic and anaerobic workouts that make her body what she wants it to be.

The idea that anaerobic exercise might be a key to health and longevity is a shocker for many people. Most think of aerobic exercise as the fountain of youth. Based on these stories and many others like them, my conclusion is that aerobic exercise is important, but not sufficient. It is a combination of aerobic and anaerobic exercise that is the most efficient path to helping you realize your potential as a runner. It is also the fountain of youth. That is what I believe.

SETTING AGE-APPROPRIATE GOALS

Lew and Ernestine are great examples of how to age gracefully. Neither one is giving up. They have both found a way to continue doing the exercise they love. They are not trying to win against younger people. They are competing with themselves, with time, with aging, and winning.

In this context, winning does not mean getting younger or getting faster. In the battle against aging, winning is to continue being capable of doing what you want to do. It is aging gracefully by working hard and smart.

Aging gracefully requires some changes in your outlook. Instead of setting a lifetime PR in the next

5K race, you set your sites on a setting a PR for the year or for the last 5 years. In Lew's case, the goal was not to be competitive & not to set a PR. Lew's goal for his last Ironman was to cross the finish line before the 12 hour cut-off.

As you get to different milestones in your life, ask yourself some key questions about your running goals. *What is the biggest goal that is achievable for someone of my age and health?* I originally had the word *reasonable* in that last sentence, but replaced it with the word *achievable*. Lew and Ernestine did not set reasonable goals by the standards of the world. They set outlandish goals and met them. Aim big; if you fail to meet a big goal, you have still done something special.

With that in mind, continue to do some research and some soul-searching:

- At this stage of my life, what should my goal be? Can I be competitive in my age group?
- Will I try for a PR for my lifetime, for the last five years or for this year?
- Is finishing enough?

Whatever goals you set will be good enough. You are the judge. Do not let anyone tell you that you are too old to run. Through your wise decisions, active lifestyle, and continuing list of achievements you will show them that your new perspective on aging gracefully is a better way to live.

"A few individuals who start running later in life or become smarter about their training can continue to improve into their 50s and even 60s, but aging cannot be postponed forever. Nevertheless, if you run and maintain a healthy lifestyle, you will look and feel a lot better than those who do not. "
--Hal Higdon

RENEWING THE GIFT: HEALTH

Along with motivation issues, health issues can also interfere with your running. This section of the book offers advice on how to keep your body running as healthy as possible. It also includes insights about when to stop running for a while to avoid major injuries.

The ideas in this section come from a combination of personal experience and reading the work of others. I am not a medical doctor, but I have learned some important things along the way that I want to share with you. ☺

> *"In running, there is more than one winner. In each runner, there is the battle to finish & many other battles along the way. Count all wins. "*
> *--P. Mark Taylor*

REST DAYS

"I love to push my body.
Recovery is the hardest part of training for me."
-- Ryan Hall

I agree with Ryan. I think rest days are the toughest ones on the schedule. I mean... well... think about it. If you think God made us to run, then our bodies should be clamoring to run. And on most days, mine is. It is screaming out with every fiber of its being. The message is loud and clear: "Go, Run, Play!"

Maybe the first and last words of that command would be okay, but my schedule says no running on Fridays. My mind says no running on Fridays. In my schedule, I need to rest before the big Saturday pace run and the long Sunday run. With no rest, these runs could go flat, or much worse things like injuries and overtraining could sideline me for a while. So, I faithfully take the day off.

Still, my body cries out: "Go, Run, Play!"

Remember This!

All runners need a day of rest periodically to recuperate from the little things, the wear and tear that running will put on your body.

Without resting periodically, we will begin to break down. Given a full day of rest, your body will thrive on a steady regimen of running.

A NOTE ABOUT RUN STREAKS

There are a lot of folks that I am friends with that do not take a full day of rest. These runners are caught up in the current trend of run streaking. No, I don't mean streaking in the sense of running without clothing. A run streak is when you run at least a mile every day for a certain length of time. The good things about run streaking are consistency and accountability. Some people that often have trouble motivating themselves to run regularly are much more motivated to get up and run if they do it every day. It instills a habit. They say habits are formed about 21 days of consistent effort. In that sense, a run streak is a very good thing.

A run streak is also good because it encourages accountability. You rarely do a run streak without reporting it daily to your running friends. Each day, you get online and Tweet or post to your friends: day 37 of the run streak! [or whatever day it happens to be] The important thing is that you report it and somebody says, "Good job! Way to stick with it!"

The downside of a run streak is in not achieving full rest. As I already pointed out, rest is about healing all of the little things, the wear and tear that running will put on your body. Given at least one full day of rest each week, the body can usually keep up. At that point, running is beneficial. Most of us cannot do a run streak for very long without having some issues arise. If you must do a run streak, then listen to your body. Do not run through bad pain. Running when you are hurting is folly, not something to be proud of.

> "The freedom of cross country is so primitive. It's woman versus nature."
> – Lynn Jennings

Take a day off when you need it. Your legs will love you for it.

"*Learning what you are made of is always time well spent.*"

NEW THOUGHTS ABOUT OLD STRETCHING

"There is an endless number of runners who seem perfectly able to squeeze in many hours of running every week but who just don't seem to have the time to stretch for five or ten minutes before and after."

-- Josh Clark

When I was young, I stretched because my coaches told me to stretch. I have never been that flexible, and I never really understood the benefits. Here are the things that we are typically told about stretching:

- Stretching prior to any type of exercise gets the muscles ready for the more intense exercise that follows.
- A well-stretched muscle moves through a full range of motion with less effort. Therefore, stretching prior to physical activity will help you conserve energy and thereby improve performance.

- Because our muscles get cold and tight from hours of sitting or standing at our jobs, periodic stretching will keep the blood flowing and allow the muscles to move through a full range of motion.
- A muscle is more flexible when it is warm and stretched, and it is less likely to tear or overstretch from an abrupt movement.
- Stretching increases the blood supply to the muscles and joints. This keeps the muscles supple and healthy.
- After a workout, stretching your muscles will keep them from immediately shortening and tightening as they cool down.

In high school, I ran both cross country and track. My cross country coach had us stretch before running and encouraged stretching after the workout. Our head track coach, however, made us run a mile first and then stretch. Both seem like pretty good ideas, but which is right? I have great respect for both of those coaches, so I am going to say that I agree with both coaches MOST of the time.

A while back, I was suffering a round of tight muscles in my calves. Over the course of a few weeks, when I stretched BEFORE the run it felt very artificial. My muscles would not stretch unless I forced them. Bad idea! They just would not budge until I pushed to the point of pain. That led to more pain and more tightness. In short, stretching a muscle that will not cooperate is a bad idea.

Does that mean that I should run without stretching? I tried. Bad idea. It just forced the muscle to stretch under duress, just like stretching before the run. That led to worse pain and increased tightness.

How do you stretch a muscle that is firmly against the idea? If stretching first is bad and stretching after a warm-up is bad... where do you go from there?

After experimenting, here is what started working for me:

- Warm up the sore muscle by slowly and carefully moving through its comfortable range first. Not by running, but just gently going through your comfortable range of motion.

- After the muscle begins to warm up, the comfortable range of motion will begin to gradually increase.
- Take that warm-up/stretch combination as far as your muscle will comfortably allow in a few minutes.
- Begin your run at an easy pace and gradually increase your speed.

This may not be new to you, but I was never told to warm up the muscle and stretch simultaneously. I suppose you could say that I am employing a combination of the advice of both of my high school head coaches. It just goes to show that the lesson that you teach to youth may be lost on them in the moment, but they can keep learning from that advice years later.

It turns out that this new form of *stretching through gentle movements* is called **dynamic stretching**. The old way of *stretching out and holding* *still while your muscles stretch* is called **static stretching**. Research comparing static and dynamic stretching shows that dynamic stretching is more beneficial. Moreover, static stretching actually hurts athletic performance. Static stretching rips muscles. Dynamic stretching liberates them. My legs told me that. The research agreed.

Now that I know this, my favorite dynamic stretches are the ones recommended by Nikki Kimball in an article in Runner's World. I found it online at:

http://www.runnersworld.com/article/0,7120,s 6-241-287--13442-0,00.html

- Leg Swings – Swing one leg back & forth in front of your body
- Butt-kicks – kick your own but with your heels while running in place
- Pike Stretch – On all fours with your butt high in the air, balance on one foot and move your heel towards the ground
- Hacky-Sack – Pretend you are trying to kick a hacky sack towards your face with the instep

of your foot. Get high enough to easily tap your instep with the opposite hand.

- Toy Soldier – Knee straight, kick one leg straight forward, high enough to easily tap your knee with your hand
- Walking lunges – talk a long stride forward, dipping down low enough to nearly touch the ground with the knee on the back leg, continue stepping forward

WHERE TO RUN: SURFACES, SITES, & TREADMILLS

"I like to choose from a wide variety of
running routes in the local parks, trails,
tracks, & roads. It makes every run
feel like a mini-vacation."

Where you run matters. Some surfaces are softer than others. That affects the impact that your legs feel. Running on solid concrete is very hard on your legs. Asphalt or blacktop seems like a hard surface, but it is much softer than concrete. My legs will notice the difference immediately because I wear minimalist shoes with no cushioning. Even in well-cushioned shoes, however, the surface will eventually make a difference. Running on concrete day after day may actually hazardous to your health. Your joints will not be as healthy as they could.

Remember This!

**Running on a variety of surfaces
will keep your legs healthier and
prepare them for races on any surface.**

A nice new track has a surface that includes rubber in the mix. This softens the landing and enables grip. The biggest problem with a track is curves. If road races were always like the track, half of each course would be a curve to the left! If you always run the same direction, your right leg will develop slightly differently than your left. Personally, I like to run at least one third of my track mileage in the opposite direction from the traditional clockwise.

What you don't get by running on a track is hills. If you live in a flat world, then that is fine. If the races you run have any hills at all, however, it is a good idea to practice running hills. If you have no hills to run, then use fartleks to mimic the change in effort that hills represent.

TRAILS & GREENWAYS

Beyond tracks and concrete or asphalt, there are trails and greenways. Sometimes a trail gets "paved" with crushed gravel. A rock road can be a nightmare to run on because you are constantly twisting your ankles a little bit. Crushed gravel, however, can make a nice even running surface that is soft enough to keep your joints happy and firm enough to run fast.

Most trail runners prefer a trail is in its natural, raw state, grass and dirt with a few rocks. If it is mostly grassy, we call it cross country. If there is little or no grass, we usually call it a trail. Either way, the runner is enjoying a very natural setting. For many runners, including myself, this is running bliss. We melt into the fold with the flowers, birds, squirrels, and other wildlife. We are doing what comes naturally to us in a very natural setting. Good times.

The drawback to trails as a running surface is the potential injury caused by uneven surfaces. If you are not watching for them, you can easily stumble on tree roots, rocks, clumps of grass, and other natural elements on the trail. The softness of the dirt and grass, however, can make up for these difficulties. If you watch where you step, trail running can be awesome!

THE PLEASURES & PERILS OF TREADMILL RUNNING

The least natural of all running surfaces, (at least in my opinion) is the treadmill. Instead of moving forward as the road stands still, on a treadmill the road moves and the runner makes an effort to stay in place. How natural is that????

The great thing about treadmill running is the climate control. In the summer, you are running in air conditioning and in the winter you are running in heat. Nice! For those that love being outdoors, the treadmill feels like a prison. For those with severe outdoor allergies, the treadmill feels like being set free. As far as comparing it to other running surfaces, treadmills tend to be a softer feel, easier on your joints.

Another thing that the treadmill has going for it is the ability to set difficulty, grade (how flat or steep), and the ability to choose workouts of varying types. Choosing the workout mode can help encourage you to follow through on your plan for the day.

Having all of the controls at your fingertips, however, can also mean that it is still easy to ease up if it feels like a bit much. One more drawback to treadmill running is pace. Seven minute miles on the treadmill are slightly easier than running seven minute miles elsewhere. One web site even has a conversion cart to guide you as you choose your treadmill pace. It shows you what the equivalent would be in other conditions. It can be found at: http://www.hillrunner.com/training/tmillchart.php

Where is the "peril" of treadmill? Well, that is a personal story. I often let my mind wander as I go for a run. Hence, I have trouble maintaining the one pace that the treadmill is going. Not staying in time with a treadmill can cause you to trip if you go too fast or to be thrown backwards if you go too slowly.

My most dangerous treadmill moment was at a gym. They had half of their treadmills and stationary bikes set up in a room with a big screen where they showed movies. Well, I made the mistake of watching the movie *Wild Hogs* for the first time while I was on a treadmill in this theater. I was running 7 minute miles when the swimming scene came up. I literally started to fall over from laughing so hard! Since the treadmill was not watching the movie with me, it had kept up the 7 minute mile pace but I had not. I was thrown to the back wall by the force of the treadmill. I have run on a treadmill only a few times since that *Wild Hog* moment, but I refuse to watch a movie or TV while I do it. ☹

> *"Will power is a muscle.*
> *The more you use it,*
> *the stronger it gets. "*

PHILOSOPHY OF PAIN

"If you feel pain at the beginning of a run
and it diminishes as you continue,
take that as a sign to keep going.
But if the pain gets worse, you'll be making a
mistake if you try to push through the pain.
Stop. Walk. Take a taxi home, if possible."
-- Hal Higdon

I am with you on this one, Hal! **Sometimes, stopping today means that you will be able to run tomorrow.** The vast majority of my improvements as a runner have come through lots of struggle and very little pain. Pain is your body telling you that something needs to change. If you have pain, find out what your body needs and make the necessary adjustments. You can run through some pains, but not others. Err on the side of caution.

So you are training for a race and you begin to feel some pain. What do you do? First, remember that pain is good. Pain is our body's way of telling us what is going on and what we might do about it. Way back in high school my coach told us about good pain and bad pain. The next paragraph is my best paraphrase of this lesson.

Good pain is muscle soreness the day after a strong workout. If you worked your tail off, your muscles have little tears that need to heal. That is why we alternate sprinting/strength days with recovery days that are relatively short and easy. Bad pain, however, is stabbing or throbbing pains that does not resemble soreness. Good pain is something to brag about because you

> "No pain, no gain.
> Is not a healthy way
> to think about running"

know that you are going to be faster and stronger when it heals. Bad pain makes you weaker, requires complete rest, and may call for some medical help.

I know how badly you want to meet your next goal, but you must listen to your body. If you are not sure whether a pain is good or bad, treat it as if it were bad. In the long run, you will meet your goal more quickly if you heed the advice your body is giving you. Better to ease up & rest up for a day or two than to make it worse and be forced to completely quit for a much longer time frame.

RICE FOR PAIN

RICE is a common guideline for when you suspect that the pain that you are feeling might be bad pain. Rice stands for Rest, Ice, Compression, & Elevation. I know that you have heard it before, but you would be amazed how many runners ignore the most basic of medical procedures until it is too late. Begin using RICE as soon as you suspect that your pain might be bad pain!

Rest is a key part of repair. Without rest, continual strain is placed on the area, leading to increased inflammation, pain, and possible further injury as well as increasing the length of time that it takes to heal. In general, the rest should be until the you are able to run with the pain essentially gone.

Ice is excellent at reducing the inflammation and the pain from heat being generated. A good method is ice 15-20 minutes of each hour for a 24–48 hour period. Always keep a piece of cloth between your skin and the ice to prevent your skin from getting frostbite. You can wrap it in a towel or just keep a layer of clothing over your skin. Be careful to not ice for too long so that your blood flow will not be too reduced to allow nutrient delivery and waste removal.

> *"Your body hears everything that your mind says.*

Compression aims to reduce the excessive swelling that results from the inflammatory process. Too much swelling results in significant loss of function, excessive pain and eventual slowing of blood flow through vessel restriction. An elastic bandage is ideal because it reduces swelling without cutting off the flow of blood that is need for recovery and normal function. The fit should be snug so as to not move freely, but still allow expansion for when muscles contract and fill with blood.

Elevation aims to reduce swelling by increasing venous return of blood to the systemic circulation. This will not only result in less swelling, but also aid in waste product removal from the area.

RICE is the old-school approach, but still useful. The one add-on I suggest is that movement is good. You don't want to exercise on a bum ankle or knee, but movement is good. A large part of physical therapy for rehabilitating injured body parts is simply taking the body carefully through all of its range of natural motions. While you are still in the using the RICE techniques, use your hands to take your injured area through the natural range of motions. If you are gentle and careful, it will increase blood flow and help you get back a little faster.

A CAUTIONARY WORD ABOUT PAIN-RELIEVERS

The use of anti-inflammatory NSAIDS such as aspirin and ibuprofen can be a healthy part of the process of reducing inflammation so that you can heal more quickly. NSAIDS and pain-relievers such as acetaminophen should NOT be used to mask the pain. You need to hear what your body is telling you!

If your pain persists for several days, it would be wise to consult your doctor. Sometimes, you need to get help in order to get back on the road as soon as possible.

> *"There is no such thing as bad weather, just soft people."*
> *--Bill Bowerman*

WEATHER AFFECTS RUNNING

"I don't want to complain about the heat,
but I think my shoe is melting."

Treadmills exist for a reason. Weather affects running. No matter how much you might want to ignore it, weather has power over us. You can't stop it. You can either work with it, or it will make you pay. In certain extremes, the cost may be your life. Weather matters. Respect it, and you can live to run another day.

As far as cold goes, most of us have the common sense to give up before temperatures get too dangerous. When the meteorologist on the local news TV or radio station is telling you something about frostbite, it is time to stay inside. Personally, I will run up to three miles when the temperature is in into the teens. I will not run long. Three miles is just long enough to maintain my fitness level.

Once the temperature drops into single digits or below, I will not go running outside. There are not significant benefits to running in such temperature as far as I'm concerned. The potential problems are huge: frostbite or death. Thankfully, I live in Knoxville, Tennessee. Hence, this dilemma rarely shows itself unless I am traveling north. The cold-weather issue for me is icy roads rather than temperature. The danger is just as real. Ice leads to falling. Falling leads to injuries and time off of training. It is better for me to wait a day or two for the ice to melt.

STAYING HEALTHY IN THE HEAT

Heat, however, is a more universal problem. It is also a sneakier problem. Some people think that they are just fine. You must realize that heat and humidity affect running pace. The pace you are capable of running at 50 degrees Fahrenheit is faster than what you are capable of running at 75 degrees. Heat combined with humidity will slow you down even more, as much as 30-60 seconds per mile depending on your fitness level. Be careful. Ease up when it gets hot.

More importantly, extreme heat kills. Extreme heat causes heat stroke. For the runners and other patrons of the great outdoors, however, there is no escaping it for very long. With a heat index over 100 degrees, how can you get in a good workout AND stay healthy?

Here are a few pointers:

Course - The right course for running on in the heat is shady. Even among shady areas, some paths are naturally cooler than others. A low-lying path next to a cool stream will be much cooler than your average route. Find a cool, shady course and it will be much easier to stay on course with your workout.

> *"Being more than two percent dehydrated in warm environments causes a decline in performance."*
> *-- Robert W. Kenefick*

Hydration - Water and sports drinks are your friends. Staying well hydrated before, during, and after a run in the heat is absolutely critical. You should be drinking water all day. Not all liquids are good for hydration. Stay away from diuretics such as caffeine, as these can dry you out and set you up for disaster.

A hydrated body functions better. If you want health and performance, you will keep your body topped off with liquids as you go. So, on a hot day, you might drink as much as a cup of water or watered down sports drink every 15 minutes. If you put it in as fast as you sweat it out, your body will thank you by staying healthy and performing as best as it can. On the other hand, it is possible to drink too much. Current recommendations are to drink to thirst. If you are thirsty, drink. If you are not thirsty, don't. Any way you handle it, make sure you have access to plenty of water and/or sports drink while you run.

You should still be careful after the run! Most of us continue sweating long after the last step of the run. Hence, it is important to keep your tank topped off! There are now quite a few choices for sports drinks to recover after the workout. The top choice remains the same as it has always been... good old water!

Acclimation - Imagine you are about to get into a really hot tub of water. Do you jump in as quickly as possible or do you ease into it slowly and get used to it. If you are smart, you choose plan B and ease into it slowly. The same idea applies to running in extreme heat. If you have been running just about every day for moths, then it is likely that you gradually acclimated to the rising temperature as summer approached. Now that it is oppressively hot, it is only a little different than what you have been doing. That is easing into it. You still have to be careful, but the heat is just not a big deal. If you have been on a treadmill every day in an air conditioned gym, however, switching to running outside can be deadly if you choose to make the switch on an oppressively hot day. Don't even think about it!

> *"It's not sweat; it's liquid awesome!"*

Worst Case Scenario: What if you were not careful? What if you ran in direct sun and failed to stay hydrated while you run outside in the heat for the first time in a long time. That could cause a heat stroke.

Cause: Extreme exertion and dehydration impair your body's ability to maintain an optimal temperature

Symptoms: Core body temp of 104 or above, headache, nausea, vomiting, rapid pulse, disorientation

Treatment: Emergency medical treatment is necessary for immediate ice-water immersion and IV-fluids

Play it safe! If it is hot, stay hydrated and go easy so you can stay healthy and survive to run hard on a cooler day. If it is below freezing, consider staying indoors so you can stay healthy and run on a warmer day.

RUNNING AND WEIGHT LOSS

"I started running to lose weight.
I kept running because it felt good."

Some people start running in order to lose weight. If this is you then I have a word of advice for you: prepare to be patient. The first thing that often happens when running to lose weight is that you gain a few pounds. How does that make sense? You gain weight at first because you are building your running muscles. That is a good thing. Muscles burn fat. In the long run those added pounds will cause you to lose weight a little faster.

The fact is that running at a relatively slow rate will not lose very much weight. A person that weighs 150 pounds that runs 5 miles in 1 hour will burn around 544 calories. That potentially represents a loss of less than one seventh of a pound. But exercise will inevitably increase your appetite. If you drink 1 bottle of sports drink and have a protein bar after your run, what have you lost? In one hour of running, you have burned burned 544 calories and consumed 300-400 calories. On the conservative end of this, you will have a net burn of 244 calories. At this rate, running for an hour every day will cause you to lose one pound every two weeks.

If this does not sound promising, it is because running is not a quick remedy for being overweight. It may work slightly faster than this since your new muscles will burn a few extra calories throughout the day, but it will be a very long road to your goal weight if running is all you do. If you planned to run for a month or two until you meet your weight goal, then running is not the right route for you. It is a lifestyle change, not a weight loss program. You can become a runner. You can lose the weight. You can be healthier. It just takes a long time. It also takes a bit more than just running.

A HEALTHY DIET

Exercise alone will not cut it. Remember my story? I lost the weight first and then started running after I had met my goal. The truth is that there is no replacement for a healthy diet. It is the only effective means of weight loss. Does a healthy diet mean that you must starve yourself? NO!

Remember This!
A healthy diet does not mean starving.
Eating a moderate amount of nutrient-rich
foods will leave you more satisfied than
eating a large amount of junk.

I am not a dietician. There are other books for that. There are, however, some commonly known "superfoods" that have been suggested for runners that qualify as nutrient-rich. If you slowly mix these into your diet, they can leave you more satisfied while eating fewer calories.

Spinach (fresh)	Sweet Potatoes
Salmon	Eggs
Blueberries *& other*	Whole grain
berries	breads/cereals
Almonds	Oranges
Walnuts	Black Beans
Quinoa	Vegetables of all sorts!

START SLOWLY & CAREFULLY

Beyond the healthy diet, you also have to consider the extra issues that being overweight will cause when starting to run regularly. No matter how much you weigh, running puts extra stress on your joints and on most of the systems in your body. That is why it is so common to hear the warning: *consult a doctor before you start an exercise program.* You need to handle this carefully and slowly.

Running WILL improve your health if you handle the transition well.

Remember This!

Eat smart.

Enter into your running program slowly. Consistent effort will pay huge dividends if you give it time.

GIVING BACK: COMMUNITY & COACHING

"There is a niche for all of us
to build on our passions to inspire each other.
Running has given me so much,
and now I want to give back to the world."
-- Joan Benoit Samuelson

I love my solo runs. In them, I find peace & relaxation. Many folks run most of their training runs alone. On the other hand, life is a team sport & running is a natural part of life. While running is primarily considered an individual sport, you quickly learn that running together holds great value. This section is focused on the community aspect of running.

*"Runners are friendly
folks in general.
It's hard to be mean
when you feel so good."*

THE RUNNING COMMUNITY

"We're brought together by our passion
for running, our goofy, endorphin-tilting
smiles and the twinkle in our eyes, as we
leap lightly as gazelles. ...okay, so we don't
all leap like gazelles. I'm sure I don't...and
if I tried, I'd probably end up bouncing
like a bunny on steroids."
-- Isabel Rivera
www.TheRunningTeacher.com

Once you start running, you will find that there is
a running community. I say that in a broad sense, but
I really mean it in lots of different ways. There are
thousands of communities across the U.S., Canada,
and the rest of the world that have formalized their
running community by forming a club. Beyond that,
however, there are informal gathering, groups, and
conversations going on everywhere. Some may meet
at the local park, but some only meet online to
discuss running and the rest of their daily lives.

Before I continue, what do I mean by community? When I say community, I mean a group of two or more people that have something in common and communicate about their shared needs & wants. The final, and in my opinion the most important, aspect that defines a community is the tendency to offer support to each other to help them meet those needs and work towards their wants. That support can be as small as one person complimenting another member of the community. That support can be as huge as the United States Track & Field Association, with all of its formal rules, rulings, and programs.

In order to help you understand the strength of the running community, I will illustrate by discussing my personal experiences at three different levels: running buddies, the local track club, and the running community I have found online.

THE LOCAL TRACK CLUB

Once a running group becomes larger, they tend to organize races and group runs. That requires an organization. In Knoxville, we call it the Knoxville

Track Club. Once I had run a 5K or two in this area, I couldn't help but notice that the same group of folks were running them. I also noticed that I would get a discount on races if I joined the club. Discount is one of my favorite words, so I signed up. I knew I would enjoy the discounts, but I was curious. Beyond the discount, what does it mean to join the track club? It doesn't take long to find out. Through the newsletters and other forms of communication, the club periodically sends out the call for volunteers to work at races. Race three, work one is the mantra. I figured that volunteering would be a good way to begin meeting other runners in the area. And it is. Volunteering to help out at local races is a great way to meet fellow runners and become a part of the local running community.

After meeting a few track club members, I began to be a bit more comfortable. Soon I found myself joining on group runs and other social events. As introverted as I am, I really look forward to running with the Sunday Morning Runners. We meet at the local greenway (running path) and start early enough that I can hang out and drink coffee with the group and still make it to church later in the morning. ☺ More importantly, this running group serves as a support group of positive encouragement. In addition to good friends, I have also found some great runners that have very helpful advice about running, racing, and life.

Members of the track club have used Facebook to communicate and now there is a group run for every day of the week. My group has coffee afterwards. Some groups are more likely to order beer when they gather after their group run. There is something for everyone. In Knoxville, a runner never lacks the opportunity for community. Good times.

There is much more to our track club, but each one is different. Find your track club or road runners club, or runners club. Whatever they choose to call it, I suggest joining it. If there isn't one where you live, start one. ☺

THE ONLINE RUNNING COMMUNITY

I have also found a very supportive community of runners online. I say community because I think of them as one group, but in fact there are many. On Facebook, I have extended my groups to include Knoxville and the world. There are countless group pages for runners. On Twitter, I am following 1,852 as of the time I am writing this. Of those 1,852 people, 1,840 are runners. I have a few triathletes and a couple of friends beyond that, but most of my Tweeps are runners. Of course there are many more runners on Twitter that I have not found, but I will eventually! Finally, I also have a community of runners on the Daily Mile web site. I use the Daily Mile to keep track of my runs, but it is also a place to share stories, pictures, questions, and advice.

What do these online communities of runners have to offer? They offer many of the same things that the local communities offer: someone with a common interest, the giving and receiving of advice and encouragement, ideas, laughs, and much more. If I want to know more about the technical aspects of running, I can post a question online and be sure that I will get several responses from experienced runners. If I scan their posts, I will often find that I

have the answers to their questions. Give and take.
That is a community.

You can find me on Twitter @Wise_Running and on
my Wise Running Facebook page at
https://www.facebook.com/WiseRunning

*"The only courage
that some people
will muster today
will come from you.
Be encouraging!"
-- P. Mark Taylor*

RUNNING BUDDIES

Runners meet to run. It happens all of the time. It is easier to get motivated to go out and run if you know someone is waiting for you. Having friends to run with provides a motivation, accountability, and miles of smiles. On an easy or long run, you can talk. If you can't talk, you might be going too fast. Your long runs, after all, should be 60 to 90 seconds per mile slower than your last 5K race pace. It is called *conversational pace* for a reason. Talk, laugh, run. It is what runners do.

If you are doing a speed or race-pace workout you might talk in between laps. Many times, people sit down for a cup of coffee or a beer after their run. Running is very much a social event with benefits including emotional and physical health. The socializing starts at the smallest level. It only takes one other runner to turn a run into a social event. Where do people find their running buddies? Good question!

I asked folks about their running buddies. On the DailyMile.com web site I posted the question,

**"Who are your running buddies
and why are they so awesome?"**

Here are a few of the responses:

- My group of friends that make up the Mount Vernon Running Buddies are awesome. We all got together and started running every morning before work after doing a local short charity race. We have fun and hold each other accountable to show up. We've logged thousands of miles and run numerous races together the past two years and I wouldn't trade it for anything.

- I have lots of running buddies. A couple I met through the DailyMile web site, most were people who were already runners and welcomed me into the fold. Each one is awesome in their own way. Most because they are faster than me and they encourage me to get better and some because running is a more productive way to catch up than getting lunch! All of them because they don't think I'm nuts.

- I have the most amazing group of running buddies! I will tell about 2 of my faves...I met Angela S. here on daily mile. She might be the most awesome person ever! Love running with her. She is so strong in every sense of the word! I also met Michaela B. thru daily mile! She is a super awesome person, runner and friend. She is so encouraging and just ridiculously fun!!! I am so thankful to call both not only running buddies, but friends!!!! Also they are both crazy like me! :)

- It's gotta be my 10-month old yellow lab, Apollo. I sometimes run with my daughter, but that's hit and miss. Apollo is always ready to go, no complaints.

- I really miss my North Dakota running buddies, such a great bunch but we keep up with each other here on DM. Being new to Tennessee I have had the pleasure to meet great local runners here on DM and actually run with some during the Knoxville Marathon and training.

But my best partner right now is my Black Lab Lady!

- Actually, my husband. It may sound a little cheesy but being that I used to be married to a sedentary (not the reason we divorced) man, I appreciate all his qualities - it's just an added bonus that we're both distance runners and share a love for fitness. He keeps me motivated and focused, and I could not ask for more in a running partner.
- The IMT Des Moines Marathon running club - I once thought I was too slow to run with others, but this group can't be beat.

If you don't have a running buddy yet, you might be wondering where to find one. I posed the question on several web sites.

How did you meet your running buddies?

Here are a few of the responses:

- At races. It's a small community here in Bangkok. You see familiar faces and start saying hi.

- I've met most run buddies through my local running club. We've met thru training classes and keep running together!
- Through my blog, DailyMile and through KTC social running events/races.
- Through work, at official runs & races, through OTHER running buddies, and on FB:) That's why I love it!!!
- Yep, what Dawn said! Oh, and sometimes at races?
- Oh! I was picturing the group training runs we have in our town - you can almost always find an organized run if you want to join one here! :)
- Through social media. Mostly Twitter (the #runKY hashtag took off last year), some Facebook...
- church/social media, other friends and events.
- We knew each other since childhood. Reconnected at a HS reunion. :)

There are your marching orders! You will find your running buddies in the highways and hedges of life. You will meet them at work, at church, at races and other local events, and online.

Remember This!

Nobody has to run alone.
Nobody has to figure it all out themselves.
People want to run through life together.
It's just easier and richer that way.

> "Learning what you are made of is always time well spent.

YOU WILL NEVER RUN ALONE

I was asking some of the folks on Facebook about encouragement one day and Brianna posted this note on the wall of my Wise Running Facebook page:

My college writing professor will be running her first marathon this week end. She is running in honor of one of her close friends who passed away from cancer recently. She told me that she wanted to finish and that her biggest worry was that her team would not be running at the same pace she would be "running alone".

At my first race before I lined up at the starting line I was given a pin that was an angel and was told "Wear this pin as a reminder that you never run alone". Those words are what got me through the every last grueling mile on that warm May Day in 2011.

I gave my professor a copy of that same prayer and to the bottom attached a pin much like the one I wore and wrote a note explaining the story of the pin and prayer. The note I had written ended with "You may not choose to wear this pin on race day but if you do, know that you never run alone".

My professor began to tear up and said that the angel would represent her lost friend and said "your right. I will never run alone" and told me that she would wear it on race day.

Today was my last class of the semester and when I walked into my College writing class on the desk where I always sit there was a book wrapped up with a bow and a card. The book was Born To Run and attached was a handmade hand written card that ended with:

"Life, like the routes you run each day, may have a roadblock thrown in every once in a while. Always remember, failures are simply reminders that no athlete or runner is ever perfect, success is not always measured in miles, and that you were born to run."

ENCOURAGING, EXHORTING &COACHING:

"Champions are everywhere;
all you need is to train them properly.

-- Arthur Lydiard

It did not take me long to figure out why running buddies and running clubs are so important. It is ten times easier to be consistent with your running when there are friendly faces there to encourage and exhort you. Doing your best comes naturally in this environment. This setting provides an excellent opportunity to give back to the running community what it has given to you. All you have to do is start encouraging the runners around you!

It does not take much effort and only a few words:

- Great job!
- Keep going!
- You are looking strong!
- You can do it!

You don't have to have the perfect words. Simply being impressed with their effort can make them smile and keep them motivated. Whether it is by words or by your demeanor, such a small effort can go a long way towards making someone's day. Once in a while, it can make the difference between giving up and continuing to try. Every positive word or phrase of encouragement counts. It is emotional fuel, so don't be stingy!

If you are going to attend a race, but not run in it then by all means, make a big sign! When you see your friends running coming towards you, jump up and down like a crazy person and tell them how awesome they are! There is a good chance that they need to hear it right then.

Even if you run the race, you can still encourage others in the race. If the course takes you past people that are faster or slower than you, cheer for them! If you get done before your friends, grab some water, take a deep breath, and walk back along the course and encourage folks as you go! It is awesome! You will love it and some of them need it. It's a win-win!

Remember this!
Running with someone may be the
encouragement they need
to get through a rough time.

Beyond racing, the grind of daily running can be a bit much for some folks too. Even the best of us have times when we are not as motivated as usual. If you are planning your runs for the next few days, consider inviting a friend to run with you. It may be what gets them to run that day instead of deciding that they are too busy. Every little encouragement matters.

FROM CHEERLEADER TO COACH

If you are an experienced runner, you have more responsibility. As with any community, the experienced folks have a knowledge base from which runners with less experience can learn. Be ready to answer questions and make positive, encouraging suggestions. Don't tell them what to do. Tell them what has worked for you and others, and allow them to decide what to do with that information. That is peer coaching. Making suggestions and giving encouragement.

If you have studied and experienced running for years, you may want to consider making the term coach a more formal arrangement. You might be able volunteer to work with local youth through the local clubs.

I personally have taken up coaching other adult runners as a hobby. I simply got on Twitter and offered to help out any runners that might want some coaching. On the first tweet, I got three responses. I had conversations with each of my new pupils and helped develop training plans to help them meet specific goals. I would check in with them every day or two to see how they were doing. It was fun for me to not only encourage but help them with the technical aspects of running. They enjoyed the expertise that I had to offer and the accountability that comes with having a coach.

On the most formal level, there is a course you can take to become a certified running coach through the Road Runners Club of America. Visit their web site at http://www.rrca.org/programs/coaching-certification/ for details.

You can also become a certified official for USA Track & Field (formerly the Athletic Congress) through their course. This is not coaching, but will allow you to be an official at youth & adult track events sanctioned by the organization. See their web site at:

http://www.usatf.org/Products---Services/Officials-Certification.aspx

OTHERS FORMS OF ENCOURAGEMENT

If you want someone to begin running, DO NOT tell them that they should run. Also, DO NOT tell them all of the benefits. Trying to convince them to run is usually not productive. After asking many runners about how to encourage a friend to run, the answer was almost unanimous: infect them with the running bug without telling them.

Stage 1: Encourage them by consistently expressing the joy and sense of accomplishment that running gives to you. The subtle approach is best, you are not trying to convince them. You are just sharing your feelings about running like you share your feelings about other things.

Stage 2: Invite them to join you on a run. Keep inviting them with no pressure attached. Perhaps one day they will join you. They may or may not. It is their decision. If you allow them the control over that decision without pressure, they are much more likely to surprise you and join you for a run one day.

Other than words of encouragement and invitation, what are some ways to encourage people to start running and then to keep running?

Let's learn some lessons from the people that support these runners:

- When I was in law school, I gained about 50 lbs in two years. My mom heard my excuses about "being on a student budget" and suggested that she would pay for any fitness/health-related expenses I incurred. I signed up for a training group, bought a pair of sneakers, registered for my first marathon, and the rest is history!

- Sometimes it is not their words of encouragement but how they are "impressed" that I run that keep me going.
- My parents help me buy new shoes when I need them but don't have a lot of money (I'm only partially employed, stupid economy).
- They think what I'm doing is so much more than it feels like to me. It keeps me going and not thinking I have to overdo. And the people in my running group - how can I measure that? Just that they keep showing up or that they say they missed me when I couldn't show and how we support each other through bad runs, hot days, cold days, injuries...

"I often hear someone say
'I'm not a real runner.'
We are all runners,
some just run faster than others.
I never met a fake runner"
-- Bart Yasso

CHARITY FUNDRAISING

Runners have big hearts. When you get as many endorphins as a dedicated runner, you tend to be happy, nice, and generous. Hence, it makes sense that one of the things that runners do fairly regularly is to raise money for charity. Races for charities are normal. I know a few runners that actually choose their races for the year by starting with a few key charity races and then filling in their schedule with other races.

Sometimes the race raises money strictly through the entry fee. In this case, you are donating to charity just by registering. You are also supporting the charity by wearing the race t-shirt, which helps the charity with name recognition on an ongoing basis. You become a walking and/or running billboard for the charity. Other races for charities may actually have you go out and collect donations as your entry fee.

The great thing about charity runs is that not only are they great for the charity, but they are also great for running. A lot of non-runners are willing to run or walk a 5K for charity when they would otherwise have no interest in running. It's a great opportunity to get your friends out for a run!

There are other forms of fundraising for runners. I have seen runners raising funds for a charity without a race attached. Some pledge to run a certain number of miles in a year if they can get 200 people to pledge a donation of $20 for the feat. The runner gets some good training and the charity of his/her choice will receive at least $400. That is a win-win!

TRAINING SCHEDULES & OTHER
RESOURCES

If you fail to plan, you are planning to fail. If you want to succeed, you must develop a plan. In this section you will find training plans for various racing distances. I have also given a quick overview of some running gear that you might want to consider as a part of your overall plan.

WHAT IS A TRAINING PLAN?

"The best way to predict the future is to create it."

-- Stephen Covey

A training plan is exactly what it sounds like. It is a plan for your training. What are you training for? In running, you train for a specific race on a specific day at a specific location. I like to race the Covenant Health Knoxville Marathon each year in spring in Knoxville, Tennessee. Each year I take a fresh look at training plans to see which plan I would like to follow to prepare me for this year's race. Sometimes I choose an 18 week plan. Once I took a 24 week plan. Which one I choose depends on the races that I am planning to run in the months before the marathon.

Training plans are usually designed by experienced runners and coaches with a few particular ideas in mind. *When it comes to training plans, however, one size does not fit all.* That is true of just about everything in running. A good shoe is not good for everyone. Likewise, a good training plan will not be good for everyone. Hence, I include my training plans with a word of caution: What works for me may or may not work for you. Take the ideas in the plan and adjust them to fit your life, your current level of training, your current level of fitness, your goals, and your schedule.

FOLLOWING MY TRAINING PLANS

That being said, what are the *ideas* in a training plan? All of my training plans have some similar features:

- An assumption about the level of the runner. At the top of each training plan, I tell you the minimum requirement for using the plan.
- A gradual increase in mileage run on a day and in the week. For the Walking to 5K plan, the amount of time spent running gradually increases. For the other plans, each type of run sees a gradual increase with a periodic decrease to rest you legs.
- An occasional race is also included in some of the plans. Usually shorter than the goal race,

these races can be considered training. They also help us measure our progress and build confidence as we approach the big race. ☺

- Rest. You may decide to rest more or less than my plan, but I believe that it should be a part of the plan. ***Rest while you are healthy.*** Do not wait to rest when you have overdone it.

- Pace is not mentioned on the plans. It is too specific to the individual to be able to include. For each type of run, follow the pacing guidelines outlined in this book in the section on Running Faster, which begins on page 25. Alternatively, you can use one of the many pace calculators on the web. I tend to use the one found at www.mcmillanrunning.com.

If you are a rookie at the goal distance, then I suggest sticking to the plan closely. If you are a returning veteran, you may want to adjust the distances some, but not too much. If it has been a while since you ran that many miles, you will need to reduce the weekly mileage to match your current weekly average and then gradually move towards the miles in the program. Stay with the workouts, but change how far you go in each one.

The workouts may not reflect your schedule. It is okay to move them around as long as you do not have intense workouts on back-to-back days. Intense workouts include the long run, intervals, fartleks, and repeats. Do your rest days and shorter runs on those days. You can rearrange the days to match your schedule, but keep it in the same week so that you can be sure that it is gradually building! It pays to set up a weekly routine so that your long runs are always 1 week apart. Consistency helps everything.

FROM WALKING TO RUNNING A 5K

Special care must be taken if you are a walker trying to run for the first time. We want this to go well. We want you to love running. It is going to be tough. If you are consistent, however, it will get easier. By the end of this program, most folks are very happy with the results.

Running can be a joy if you stick to the program. There is no point where you run on back to back days in this program. That is an advanced move. After you graduate from this program and complete a 5K running the whole way, then you can begin to add more running days if you would like. For now, please stick to the three days with running and three days of walking.

Another critical feature is the walking days. These do not represent a saunter through the park. These are serious work days at a quick pace. Just because they are walking, it is not okay to skip them. The brisk walking days will help you work out any soreness created on the running days. They will help you succeed at running.

The running days are critical as well. The time spent running gradually increases and the time spent walking decreases. Stick with the program. With the change each week, the beginning of the week will be the hardest part. The workout should get easier throughout the week. Not easy, just easier.

Warning!!! Do not get ahead of the program just because you feel pretty good one day. You may feel fine today, but go too far too fast and you might be so sore tomorrow that you never want to run again. If you stick closely to the program and let the changes be small and consistent, you will gradually feel yourself being transformed.

How fast should you run on the running days? Slowly!! We are not training to be the fastest runner in the park. We are gently teaching our body to run. I recommend that you not keep track of how fast you are going. I recommend that you lightly jog. I spend most of my time running much slower than I would in a race. Follow my lead and be happy just to run. Patience now means happy running later.

In your first 5K race, happily do a light run from start to finish. If you want to get faster, we can work on that later. It is possible that you may feel the need to walk a little in your first 5K. That is okay. You are still out getting it done. You are gradually removing your limitations. You rock! I will be proud and happy to see you step over the threshold and become a runner. It does not happen on race day. It happens on day two of the program. It happens on the first step of the first thirty second job. Welcome to the club; we are glad to see you here!

"Some people reduce fitness to a look, and even find comfort thinking it's all vanity, but the truth is when you take care of yourself from the inside out you gain an inner confidence and self-respect that helps you to continue on this fitness path."
-- Kim Dolan Leto

TRAINING - WALKING TO RUNNING A 5K - *For those already comfortable walking a 5K.*

Week	Sun	Mon	Tues	Wed	Thurs	Fri	Sat
1	Walk 3 miles briskly	2 Miles Total = walk 5 minutes, then alternate between running for 30 seconds and walking for 2 minutes	Walk 3 miles briskly	2 Miles Total = walk 5 minutes, then alternate between running for 30 seconds and walking for 2 minutes	Walk 4 miles briskly	Rest	2 Miles Total = walk 5 minutes, then alternate between running for 30 seconds and walking for 2 minutes
2	Walk 3 miles briskly	2.5 Miles Total = walk 5 minutes, then alternate between running for 45 seconds and walking for 2 minutes	Walk 3 miles briskly	2.5 Miles Total = walk 5 minutes, then alternate between running for 45 seconds and walking for 2 minutes	Walk 5 miles briskly	Rest	2.5 Miles Total = walk 5 minutes, then alternate between running for 45 seconds and walking for 2 minutes
3	Walk 3 miles briskly	3 Miles Total = walk 5 minutes, then alternate between running for 1 minute and walking for 2 minutes	Walk 3 miles briskly	3 Miles Total = walk 5 minutes, then alternate between running for 1 minute and walking for 2 minutes	Walk 5 miles briskly	Rest	3 Miles Total = walk 5 minutes, then alternate between running for 1 minute and walking for 2 minutes
4	Walk 3 miles briskly	3 Miles Total = walk 5 minutes, then alternate between running for 1.5 minutes & walking for 2 minutes	Walk 3 miles briskly	3 Miles Total = walk 5 minutes, then alternate between running for 1.5 minutes & walking for 2 minutes	Walk 5 miles briskly	Rest	3 Miles Total = walk 5 minutes, then alternate between running for 1.5 minutes & walking for 2 minutes

Week							
5	Walk 3 miles briskly	3 Miles Total = walk 5 minutes, then alternate between running for 2 minutes & walking for 2 minutes	Walk 3 miles briskly	3 Miles Total = walk 5 minutes, then alternate between running for 2 minutes & walking for 2 minutes	Walk 5 miles briskly	Rest	3 Miles Total = walk 5 minutes, then alternate between running for 2 minutes & walking for 2 minutes
6	Walk 3 miles briskly	3 Miles Total = walk 5 minutes, then alternate between running for 2 minutes & walking for 1 minute	Walk 3 miles briskly	3 Miles Total = walk 5 minutes, then alternate between running for 2 minutes & walking for 1 minute	Walk 5 miles briskly	Rest	3 Miles Total = walk 5 minutes, then alternate between running for 2 minutes & walking for 1 minute
7	Walk 3 miles briskly	3 Miles Total = walk 5 minutes, then alternate between running for 2.5 minutes & walking for 30 seconds	Walk 3 miles briskly	3 Miles Total = walk 5 minutes, then alternate between running for 2.5 minutes & walking for 30 seconds	Walk 5 miles briskly	Rest	3 Miles Total = walk 5 minutes, then alternate between running for 2.5 minutes & walking for 30 seconds
8	Walk 3 miles briskly	3 Miles Total = walk 5 minutes, then run the rest of the way	Walk 3 miles briskly	3 Miles Total = walk 5 minutes, then run the rest of the way	5 minute Walk and then run 1 mile	Rest	5 minute walk for warmup & then **Run a 5K RACE**

TRAINING TO RACE A 5K - *For those who are already comfortable running a 5K.*

Week	Sun	Mon	Tues	Wed	Thurs	Fri	Sat
1	5 miles	1 mile EZ	3 miles	3 mile tempo	3 miles	Rest	800m intervals
2	5 miles	1 mile EZ	3 miles	400 m repeats	3 miles	Rest	3 mile Fartleks
3	5 miles	1 mile EZ	3 miles	3 mile tempo	3 miles	Rest	800m intervals
4	6 miles	1 mile EZ	3 miles	400 m repeats	4 miles	Rest	5K RACE
5	6 miles	1 mile EZ	3 miles	4 mile tempo	4 miles	Rest	4 mile Fartleks
6	7 miles	1 mile EZ	3 miles	400 m repeats	4 miles	Rest	800m intervals
7	7miles	1 mile EZ	3 miles	4 mile tempo	4 miles	Rest	5 mile Fartleks
8	5 miles	1 mile EZ	3 miles	3 mile tempo	Rest	Rest	5K RACE

TRAINING TO RACE A 10K - *For those who are already comfortable racing a 5K.*

Week	Sun	Mon	Tues	Wed	Thurs	Fri	Sat
1	5 miles	1 mile EZ	3 miles	3 mile tempo	3 miles	Rest	800m intervals
2	6 miles	1 mile EZ	3 miles	400 m repeats	3 miles	Rest	3 mile Fartleks
3	7 miles	1 mile EZ	3 miles	3 mile tempo	4 miles	Rest	800m intervals
4	8 miles	1 mile EZ	4 miles	400 m repeats	4 miles	Rest	**5K RACE**
5	4 miles	1 mile EZ	4 miles	4 mile tempo	5 miles	Rest	4 mile Fartleks
6	9 miles	1 mile EZ	4 miles	400 m repeats	5 miles	Rest	800m intervals
7	10miles	1 mile EZ	4 miles	4 mile tempo	4 miles	Rest	5 mile Fartleks
8	5 miles	1 mile EZ	3 miles	3 mile tempo	Rest	Rest	**10K RACE**

TRAINING PLAN: HALF MARATHON *For those already comfortable running at least 6 miles.*

Week	Sun	Mon	Tues	Wed	Thurs	Fri	Sat
1	5 miles	Rest or Cross-Train	3 miles	3 mile tempo	3 miles	Rest	800m intervals
2	6 miles	Rest or Cross-Train	3 miles	400 m repeats	3 miles	Rest	3 mile Fartleks
3	7 miles	Rest or Cross-Train	3 miles	3 mile tempo	3 miles	Rest	800m intervals
4	8 miles	Rest or Cross-Train	3 miles	400 m repeats	3 miles	Rest	10K RACE
5	5 miles	Rest or Cross-Train	4 miles	4 mile tempo	4 miles	Rest	4 mile Fartleks
6	9 miles	Rest or Cross-Train	4 miles	400 m repeats	4 miles	Rest	800m intervals

Week							
7	10miles	Rest or Cross-Train	4 miles	5 mile tempo	4 miles	Rest	5 mile Fartleks
8	11 miles	Rest or Cross-Train	4 miles	400 m repeats	2 miles	Rest	10K or 10 miles RACE
9	5 miles	Rest or Cross-Train	5 miles	5 mile tempo	4 miles	Rest	800m intervals
10	12 miles	Rest or Cross-Train	5 miles	400 m repeats	4 miles	Rest	5 mile Fartleks
11	12 miles	Rest or Cross-Train	5 miles	5 mile tempo	4 miles	Rest	800m intervals
12	10 miles	Rest	5 miles	3 mile Tempo	1 mile	Rest	Half Marathon

TRAINING PLAN: MARATHON - *For those already comfortable racing a half marathon.*

Week	Sun	Mon	Tues	Wed	Thurs	Fri	Sat
1	9 miles	1 mile or Cross-Train	3 miles	3 mile tempo	3 miles	Rest	800m intervals
2	10 miles	1 mile or Cross-Train	3 miles	400 m repeats	3 miles	Rest	3 mile Fartleks
3	5 miles	1 mile or Cross-Train	3 miles	3 mile tempo	3 miles	Rest	800m intervals
4	11 miles	1 mile or Cross-Train	3 miles	400 m repeats	3 miles	Rest	**10K RACE**
5	12 miles	1 mile or Cross-Train	4 miles	4 mile tempo	4 miles	Rest	4 mile Fartleks
6	7miles	1 mile or Cross-Train	4 miles	400 m repeats	4 miles	Rest	800m intervals
7	13 miles	1 mile or Cross-Train	4 miles	5 mile tempo	4 miles	Rest	5 mile Fartleks
8	14 miles	1 mile or Cross-Train	4 miles	400 m repeats	2 miles	Rest	**Half Marathon**
9	5 miles	1 mile or Cross-Train	5 miles	5 mile tempo	4 miles	Rest	800m intervals

Training Schedules & Other Resources

Week							
10	15 miles	2 miles	5 miles	8 miles	4 miles	Rest	5 mile Fartleks
11	17 miles	2 miles	7 miles	5 mile tempo	4 miles	Rest	800m intervals
12	18 miles	2 miles	5 miles	3 mile Tempo	1 mile	Rest	**10K RACE**
13	12 miles	2 miles	7 miles	8 miles	4 miles	Rest	6 miles at Goal Pace
14	20 miles	2 miles	5 miles	4 mile tempo	4 miles	Rest	5 mile Fartleks
15	14 miles	2 miles	7 miles	8 miles	4 miles	Rest	6 miles at Goal Pace
16	20 miles	2 miles	5 miles	4 mile tempo	4 miles	Rest	5 mile Fartleks
17	14 miles	2 miles	4 miles	8 miles	4 miles	Rest	8 miles
18	10 miles	2 miles	4 miles	3 miles	Rest	Rest	1-2 miles
Marathon Sunday!							

THE RIGHT STUFF: RUNNING TOOLS & SUPPLIES

"Running gear doesn't make the runner,

but the wrong gear can break a runner."

A recent study showed that amateur cyclists that bought fancy equipment actually improved more quickly than equivalent cyclists. Did the gear do this? Probably not. Equipment does not change the capacity or fitness of your body. One of the possible explanations for this, however, does make sense. Those that wore top notch cycling gear would actually feel a little silly if they didn't take the sport seriously. There seemed to be an incentive to train just a little harder to prove that they belong in the equipment.

Having the right stuff is crucial, but what do you really need? This is a matter of opinion. I will shares with you my list of things I believe all runners actually need, what items are nice to have, and what to get if you can afford it.

WHAT RUNNERS ACTUALLY NEED

My list of things that you actually need to be a runner is very short and driven by health. I believe that all you need to be a runner is a good pair of shoes, some clothes that keep you comfortable, and a stopwatch. That is it. Finding the first two things on the list, however, of running gear can get tricky!

A good pair of running shoes to me would be a horrible pair of running shoes for many runners. If you have been running for a while, you probably already know what you like. *A good policy for running shoes is to stick to what works.* The latest trend should not define what you put on your feet. Shoes that keep you comfortable on a run of any distance are to be considered golden! Unfortunately, every once in a while, the shoe maker will "improve" your favorite shoes or just stop making them. This is a sad day. It means that you have to go back and do some experimenting to find a new shoe that works.

If you do not know what will work for you, then follow the advice that I gave to the newbie runners:

Go to your nearest running store. Do not go to a sporting goods store, a department store, or a discount store. Go to your nearest running store. The workers there run. They are runners. They want you to enjoy running and they have a way of analyzing your needs and helping you select a good shoe to get you started. You can go discount or online AFTER you have found your good running shoes. For the first round, have the experts help you choose and reward them for their effort by buying the shoes from their store.

It may take a few tries before you find the pair that makes you the most comfortable. Keep going back to the experts, tell them what you liked and didn't like. They will treat you right and be right most of the time.

Beyond shoes, there are the **basic clothing items**. Most runners wear socks, shorts, supportive undergarments, t-shirts, and an assortment of winter gear. With all of this clothing, you will need to do some experimenting. Don't buy more than one of anything until you have road-tested it on your runs for a week. Just like shoes, you will eventually find your favorite.

Spiffy looking clothes are nice, but sometimes they can cause chaffing. I strongly recommend that you select and wear the best looking clothing from among the items that are the most comfortable. Lots of running gear is made to look snappy, so you should be able to find a balance between looks and comfort. One more detail: every item you wear should wick sweat away from your body. Most clothing designed for runner are already made of wicking fabric. Double-check that before you buy.

The shoes & clothing will get you on the road and running, but if you have set goals that have to do with time, you are going to need a stopwatch. My digital **wristwatch with a stopwatch** feature costs about $12 at your local discount store. If you are going to time yourself on a path that is already measured and marked for you, then that this inexpensive timing device is as fancy as you need to get to work towards your goals.

ITEMS THAT ARE NICE TO HAVE

I ran for several years with just a stopwatch and proceeded to meet many goals and climb the ladder in my age group results at local races. At a certain point, however, I began to see the limitations of the simple wristwatch. I was in a half marathon race when I became very frustrated. I didn't know how fast or slow I was going until I got to the next mile marker and then did the math to find out how long that mile took me to complete. I was frustrated!

The answer to that dilemma is the first item on my "Nice to Have" list. **A GPS watch**. A running watch with GPS gives a lot of information. The most critical piece of information is my current pace. By current, it means the pace that you have been running over the last 10 to 15 seconds. It is less than perfect in accuracy, but it is a lot better than running blind! For the data-driven runner, the GPS is a great blessing. Beyond the current pace, it gives you the distance run, elapsed time, lap pace, lap time, and much more.

Living in the foothills of the Smoky Mountains, the elevation gain and loss is also critical information provided by the GPS watch. Here is a graph of the elevation of a recent 5 mile race. ☺

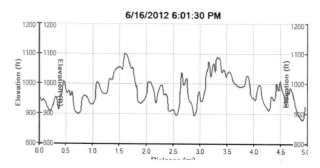

Many GPS watches are also paired with a **heart monitor**. Fitness gurus track heart rate as a measure of the effort that should be done in exercise. This too can guide your running efforts. I have not explored this one fully myself, which is why I have not covered it in this book.

Hydration is always an issue, so I have a **hydration belt** in which I carry four 8 ounce water bottles. It also has two large pockets to allow me to carry energy gels and band-aids. I do not bother wearing my hydration belt on runs shorter than 8 miles. You may have different needs. Some runners do not run a single mile without carrying water. Others don't carry water at all. If so, those runners would have to carefully plan their runs to have access to water!

A wide variety of **safety reflective gear** is available at your local running stores and cycling stores. Even in a relatively well-lit area, darkness can leave a runner unseen by a driver. I have slap-on wristbands that I wear if I run on the roads at night. I also have a reflective vest for when I go in darker areas. At first I felt kind of silly going to this extreme. After a while, I realized that the cars notice me much sooner in fully reflective running gear. Better safe than sorry!

A good **running headlamp** is also a good safety tool for runners that run before sunup or after the sun sets. Yes, folks, there is a headlamp that you strap to your head. A strong headlamp will help you see the road and avoid potholes and obstacles. Even if you end up with a weak headlamp, wear it. It may not help you see very well but it still helps you be seen by drivers!

One last item makes my short list of items I suggest for runners: **electrolyte supplements**! While it is possible to get enough electrolytes through the food you eat, I am just not that careful about my food. As runners in the summertime, we sweat. We sweat a lot. Sometimes after a run, I will go in the air conditioning and continue to sweat for twenty minutes. It is kind of gross! With every drop of sweat you are losing electrolytes, the minerals that enable our nervous system to act properly.

When you run out of electrolytes, your muscles cramp, hard. In the winter, I can get by on sports drinks and careful eating, but as soon as spring rolls around, I need my electrolyte supplements. You can buy tablets that dissolve in water, you can buy capsules that you swallow with water, or you can buy powder to add to water. Water plus electrolyte supplement equals reduced likelihood of cramping.

For some reason, I need more electrolyte supplements than the average runner. Like most other things about running, I figured this out by trial and error. Error can hurt sometimes, but I eventually figure it out. Then it is back to the bliss of running. Good times. Happy Running!

> *"You get what you expect.*
> *Believe in your dreams."*
> *-- Thomas Kennedy*

WRAPPING UP THE GIFT

Obviously, this book is just a start. This is enough to get you going and then help you get faster. There is so much more to learn about running. The learning process itself can be fun. Read a lot. Run a lot. Talk a lot about your running and reading about running.

I will keep posting new things that I learn on my blog, on Twitter, and on Facebook.

My blog is found at: *http://www.wiserunning.com*

Train hard, race easy.

Enjoy the gift of running!

End Notes

Made in the USA
Middletown, DE
27 March 2015